# BIRDING FOR BEGINNERS

# BIRDING FOR BEGINNERS

## Sheila Buff

LYONS & BURFORD, PUBLISHERS

Design by Catherine Lau Hunt

Printed in the United States of America

10 9 8 7 6 5 4 3

Library of Congress Cataloging-in-Publication Data

Buff. Sheila.
    Birding for beginners/Sheila Buff.
        p.     cm.
    Includes index.
    ISBN 1-55821-209-4
    1. Bird watching.     I. Title.
OLG77.5.B793      1993
598'.07234—dc20                                          93-3599
                                                           CIP

# CONTENTS

· · · · · · · · · · · · ·

Appendices

# Introduction

· · · · · · · · · · · · · · · ·

*T*his is a book for beginning birdwatchers, written by someone who considers herself no more than an advanced beginner. So much of what experienced birders take for granted is brand-new to beginners, who find themselves bewildered by jargon, mystified by basic identification, and frustrated by their inability to find birds to watch. The goal of *Birding for Beginners* is to present, in a calm and reassuring manner, the sort of basic information that people just getting started in birdwatching need.

As so many birding books inexplicably do, this book has a bias toward the northeastern United States. More specifically, it is biased toward the Hudson Valley, where the author does most of her birdwatching. Although the examples tend to be based on the birds common there, the basic principles should be universally applicable. The great Louis Pasteur, originator of the modern scientific method, once said, "In the fields of observation, chance favors the prepared mind." If you understand the simple logic of bird families, habitats, and field observation, you will see more birds and identify them more readily.

The chapters of this book are arranged in a sequence appealing to the perspective of someone very new to birdwatching. Thus, the book begins not with identification techniques but with a chapter on simply finding birds to identify. From there, it discusses that essential tool, the field guide. Basic information on bird identification through appearance, song, habitat, and behavior is found in chapters 3 through 6; the joys and pitfalls of listing are discussed in chapter 7. Chapter 8 is a long, but important, chapter on optics for birders. In chapter 9, the basics of an enjoyable day in the field are covered. The last chapter and the appendices detail how and where to learn more about birds. Birders tend to be systematic and logical, but there is no particular need to read this book in chapter order.

Beginners, especially those taking up the pursuit of birds as older adults, need to keep their perspective. What matters on a birding trip is not that you see a lot of different or unusual birds, or that you see more of them than anyone else — what matters is that you have an enjoyable time appreciating the natural world. Improved identification skills and a longer life list will come naturally as you gain experience. In the meantime, do the best you can and have fun.

Of all the many satisfactions birdwatching offers, perhaps the most profound is an intense appreciation of the vast, enormously complex web of nature. In recent years, birders have become deeply aware of how easily the fragile fabric of that web can be irreparably torn. The birds that were once so abundant in North America that passing flocks darkened the skies are today vanishing with distressing speed, victims of habitat destruction and fragmentation both here and in Central and South America. As the birds disappear, our natural heritage of beauty and life is also being destroyed forever. If we are to have birds to watch in the future, we must act now to preserve the planet we share with them.

# Finding and Watching Birds

· · · · · · · · · · · · · · · · · · · · · · · · · · · · · · · · · · · · ·

The most important requirement for becoming a proficient bird-watcher is something you have already: enthusiasm for the natural world. All you need to do is take that enthusiasm, grab your binoculars, step outdoors, and start looking.

## BIRDS ALL AROUND

As you get started in birdwatching, you may come to the startling realization that you have always been surrounded by birds and never really knew it. The simplest way to find birds to watch is to look in your own backyard. In a typical urban or suburban yard (or park or other open area), you will routinely see several obvious and easily identified common species, including house (English) sparrows, rock doves (pigeons), starlings, robins, blue jays, and perhaps a few more.

If you put up a bird feeder or a birdbath, you will attract more and different birds to observe. But doesn't that mean that the birds were there all along? Yes—you simply weren't looking for them. Now that you know they're there, practice your birding techniques on them.

One really satisfying aspect of birdwatching is that the more you watch, the more you see. The more often and more carefully you look at the familiar birds in your backyard, the better you will get to know them and how they behave. You may even learn to recognize individual birds among several of the same species. You will also start to see additional species because you have learned to differentiate among similar birds. For example, the small, brownish birds that you previously lumped together as just sparrows will resolve themselves into distinct species. And when a slightly different sparrow-like bird turns up, you will realize that it is a new bird for you and you will be able to pin down its identity. Most amazing of all, new birds will seem to occur more often because you have begun to look more carefully at all the birds you see.

The most common birds are also the most important to know really well, since they are often the benchmarks for descriptions and comparisons. Birds are often described as being about the size of a sparrow, robin, crow, or other common bird, for example. The better you know the common birds, the better you will be able to identify related birds, and the better you will understand the differences among birds. The same behavior patterns you see in backyard birds can be seen, with minor variations, in birds anywhere. Once you learn to recognize aggressive behavior in a tufted titmouse at your feeder, for example, you will probably be able to recognize that behavior in other birds in different feeding situations.

## HABITAT AND NICHE

Moving beyond your immediate neighborhood, where are the birds? Try looking in any open area with vegetation, especially one with water: fields, vacant lots, parks, wooded areas, streambeds, and fields near airports. Even if you live in an urban area, there's bound to be some open space around you. Central Park, in the heart of densely urban Manhattan, is an oasis for birds. More than 250 species have been sighted there, while more than 300 species have been seen at Jamaica Bay Wildlife Refuge, quite literally in the shadow of Kennedy International Airport. Peregrine falcons have been feeding on complacent pigeons and nesting successfully on the 37-story USF&G building in downtown Baltimore since 1977; peregrines also nest on large suspension bridges and skyscrapers in other East Coast cities, including New York.

Going a little farther afield, get to know the more obscure corners of your area. Abandoned railroad tracks, landfills and dumps, sewage treatment plants, and other attractive (to birds) sites are excellent places for spotting birds. Admittedly, breathing in the aroma of a sewage settling pond is not everyone's idea of a good time, but don't let peer pressure stop you. Look forward to the time when you can visit the Brownsville dump in the Rio Grande Valley to see Mexican crows.

What are you really doing as you wander around town peering into drainage canals and gazing up into trees? You are looking for birds in a variety of ecological habitats and niches — and the more habitats and niches you explore, the more birds you will see.

The concepts of range, habitat, and niche are crucial to finding and understanding birds. Broadly speaking, the range is the geographic area in which a species is found. Some species are resident year-round in their range; migratory birds have winter and breeding ranges. Within the range, birds occupy habitats and ecological niches.

A bird's range often encompasses a variety of geographic features and plant communities. Within its range, a particular bird will usually be found only in its preferred habitat, or particular combination of terrain and vegetation. Some birds are commonly found in broadly defined habitats such as mixed deciduous woodlands; others are found only in very restricted habitats such as large stands of jack pines, six to eighteen feet tall in north-central Michigan (the rare Kirtland's warbler).

Within a habitat, particular birds can reliably be found occupying particular niches. A bird's niche is the role it plays within the habitat: where and how it lives, nests, finds food, and does everything else. The classic example of how niches work is the bill length of various shorebirds. Sanderlings, which have short, slightly stubby bills, are found in the same habitat as long-billed curlews, which have long, slender bills some nine inches long. These birds can share the same habitat because they occupy different niches within it: the sanderling feeds on tiny crustaceans it finds just below the surface of the sand right where the waves wash in and out; the long-billed curlew feeds on worms it pulls from deep burrows in mud flats.

From the above discussion, it is clear that different birds are found in different habitats, and that the way to find birds to watch

Manuel F. Cheo

*The shorebird lineup from bottom to top, the birds shown here are: semipalmated plover, sanderling, red knot, greater yellowlegs, marbled godwit, and long-billed curlew. Sadly, in real life the birds never arrange themselves so conveniently.*

is to visit their habitats. The area where habitats come together —
where woodland meets with open fields, for example — is called an
ecotone. Because ecotones contain mixed habitats, they also contain
mixed bird life. Thus, ecotones tend to have more birds of more
species than do individual habitats. Among birders, this is known as
the edge effect. One good way to see more birds is to seek out
edges and mixed habitats.


## WHERE TO GO

Fortunately for birdwatchers and other nature lovers, North
America contains a wide variety of easily accessible habitats open to
the public. The birds are found in the thousands of parks, wildlife
refuges and reserves, wilderness areas, bird sanctuaries, and other
natural spots at the national, state, provincial, and municipal levels.
In addition, sanctuaries and refuges covering thousands of acres are
owned and operated by nonprofit organizations such as the National Audubon Society and The Nature Conservancy.

A really good way to see birds in the company of more experienced birdwatchers is to join your local birding club. The friendly
and enthusiastic members of the club will have regularly scheduled
evening meetings devoted to slide shows, discussions, and the occasional guest speaker; they will also have regularly scheduled field
trips to local sites. Bird clubs also often organize field trips to more
distant places, arranging for carpools or buses and lodging.

If you are new to birding, you may not know if there is a club
in your area, but there almost certainly is. To find out, ask around
and do a little detective work. Ask the people you meet while
birding locally; ask your local librarian; ask your local or state
wildlife authorities (speak to the nongame biologist). Check the

events calendar of your local newspaper—bird walks and field trips sponsored by the club will probably be listed, especially in the spring. If the local paper has a birding column (many do), call the author.

One of the very best ways to see a lot of different birds in a short time is to visit a birding hot spot during migration periods. Hot spots are places where birds congregate in large numbers and in great variety. An internationally famous hot spot is Cape May in New Jersey. During the spring and fall migrations, many birds follow the Atlantic coast flyway. If they are headed south, they often land at Cape May at the tip of New Jersey to rest, feed, and await favorable weather before taking off to cross the open water of Delaware Bay. Conversely, if they are headed north, the birds land at Cape May after flying over Delaware Bay.

There are numerous other hot spots in North America, as well as thousands of other good places to bird. Books discussing—often in very specific detail—places to go and what you are likely to see are called finding guides. On the local level, finding guides may cover only a county or even just a municipality. Guides have been published detailing good birding sites for virtually every state and province, while additional guides cover regions such as New England or the lower Colorado River valley. An excellent selection of finding guides is available through the American Birding Association (see Appendix B).

When you arrive at a birding site—a wildlife refuge, for example—always stop at the visitors' center first, where you may pay an entrance fee or make a modest contribution, get a checklist and a map, and chat with anyone who is there. Ask about what birds are being seen in various locations. If there is a sighting book, take a look at the entries from the past few days. Other birding visitors may have noted interesting birds and where they were seen.

Finally, always use the restroom facilities — there probably won't be any in the field.

## SPOTTING BIRDS

Beginners often don't see many birds even when they get to where the birds are. The birds are there — you just need some basic pointers and a lot of practice.

Start by simply trying to *see* birds — not necessarily to identify them. Go birdwatching when the birds are most likely to be active: the first few hours from dawn on, or the last couple of hours before dusk. In woods, fields, and parks, on paths and along roadsides, walk slowly and quietly, holding your binoculars lightly with both hands. Avoid sudden movements, pointing, and loud noises. Keep alert for telltale motion in the vegetation. If you see some leaves rustle, or catch the motion of a flitting bird out of the corner of your eye, stand still and look carefully at the suspect area. If you see the bird or see movement, keep your eyes fixed on the spot. Bring your binoculars up to your eyes with both hands and focus. If you can't see the bird, but are sure you are focused on the right spot (more or less), scan back and forth around the area, starting at the top and working your way down. (Don't scan in circles — you'll make yourself dizzy.) The chances are good that the bird is still somewhere nearby. On the other hand, there's a reasonable chance that what you saw was simply the very common "falling-leaf" bird.

You will need to practice the technique of bringing your binocs up smoothly without taking your gaze off the bird. To avoid serious frustration, practice this at your backyard feeder or on the pigeons in a park until it becomes second nature.

If you think you are scaring the birds away, try disguising your presence by leaning against a tree trunk or squatting behind a bush.

Don't give up too quickly — if you want to see the bird, you may have to wait several minutes or even longer. On the other hand, don't linger too long if you're pretty sure the bird has flown or if you start to feel your frustration level rising.

Listen for birdsong and calls; also listen for rustling and scratching noises. Particularly in the spring, birds often perch on high points to proclaim their territories (a classic example is a meadowlark singing from a fencepost in a field). If you hear a bird, stand still and try to pinpoint the sound, or at least its general direction. Scan the area with your binocs and try to spot the bird. If you hear a song, scan projecting branches, the tops of trees and bushes, fenceposts, and overhead wires. If you hear calls or feeding noises (the sound of a rufous-sided towhee scratching up dead leaves on the forest floor, for example), scan lower down. Often, a bird stops singing or calling when it sees people. If this happens, stand still and wait. The bird will very likely resume singing in a few minutes. Once you've spotted a singing bird, keep looking. Other birds — particularly a female of the same species — may be nearby.

Check around ponds, lakes, and wet, brushy areas such as streambeds — the trees and vegetation can abound in warblers in the spring, and birds such as spotted sandpipers and Louisiana waterthrushes can often be found on the ground.

Look up. Scan the sky for hawks and other birds. Scan overhead wires, TV antennas, and rooftops. It is astonishing how many people never notice anything that is above eye level, unless it is specifically pointed out to them. (Black vultures by the dozen can be seen perched broodingly on the roof of the huge vehicle assembly building at the Kennedy Space Center, yet busload after busload of tourists fail to notice them.) Try to follow the paths of flying birds and note where they alight. Often, a flying bird moves only a short distance. It may flit from one branch to another, or dart out to grab an insect and return to its original spot or one nearby. As you scan the sky or follow the movement of a flying bird, be aware of the sun's location. Don't look at the sun through your binoculars.

Always look carefully at *all* the birds in a group or flock of birds. A small flock of one warbler species may have a few other warblers or other birds mixed in; a group of what seem to be identical sandpipers may in fact contain several different species.

In woodlands and fields, you can try another technique: let the birds come to you. Dress warmly—you will be sitting still for a long time. Bring along something waterproof to sit on, something to drink, your binoculars, and your notebook. Find a likely spot— an open area at the base of a large tree, for example—and settle down to see what comes your way. After you have been sitting quietly for five or ten minutes, the birds will begin to go about their business while ignoring you. Within twenty minutes, you could easily find yourself looking a chickadee or a yellow warbler in the eye.

Shorebirds and waterfowl in wetlands and coastal regions are a little easier to spot, since they are usually out in the open. The best way to see these birds is to visit a refuge area. Many of these sites have trails, roads, or boardwalks specifically designed to provide good viewing with a minimum of effort. If the site has a loop road along the dikes used for water-level management, you can drive conveniently from turnout to turnout.

To see shorebirds when they are feeding and most active, try to time your visit to coincide with low tide, when mud flats and the beach are exposed. At high tide, the birds tend to huddle together and not do much of anything. If you can't find a tide listing near the weather map in the local paper, call the site and ask.

In addition to looking for birds swimming in the water or standing on the mud flats or shoreline, be sure to scan the tops of the vegetation for songbirds. Scan along the base of the phragmites for elusive birds such as rails. (Phragmites, or phrags for short, is the very tall, dense, reedy grass with a feathery top that makes up the dominant vegetation at many wetlands sites.)

If the site has an observation tower, climb it. This is a good way to grasp the lay of the land, watch birds in flight, see birds that are floating off shore, and appreciate the size of large flocks of birds.

Some sites have blinds set up at convenient observation points. The shelter of a blind is particularly welcome in windy and wet weather. Blinds are useful whenever concealment is needed for spotting shy birds, watching nest sites, and the like. When you are inside a blind, stay back a bit from the viewing window — the birds will see you if you put your face directly into the opening. Move and speak quietly. Be sure to close the window covers and door properly when you leave, and obey any other injunctions that may be posted in the blind.

## PISHING

All too often, the birds you want to see are lurking out of sight, hidden in foliage or undergrowth. You can often get the birds to appear, at least briefly, by making noises to attract them.

Pishing (or spishing) is the technique of attracting birds with a rhythmic hissing, "pishing," or "spishing" noise made by inhaling and exhaling loudly through closed teeth while simultaneously moving the lips. At its tamest, pishing sounds much like the hissing noise customarily used to call cats. Enthusiastic pishers manage to produce a loud, wheezy, sustained noise with lots of harmonic overtones in it. One word of advice: Don't talk about pishing into the bushes in polite (i.e., nonbirding) company.

To pish effectively, position yourself inconspicuously near a likely spot — a brushy area near a stream, for example. Pish loudly and long, keeping the noise up for several minutes or until you run out of breath and get dizzy. Especially during migration periods, you are likely to attract birds of several species to the area around you. Some birds respond better to pishing than others. Chickadees, catbirds, kinglets, nuthatches, sparrows, thrushes, and warblers are particularly quick to respond, but other birds such as jays and woodpeckers may also appear. Pishing is an excellent way to get the warblers that are darting around in the woods and undergrowth to pop out where they can be seen. You will hear alarm chirps and rustlings, and then start seeing the birds. Have your binoculars at the ready.

An alternative to pishing is to make squeaking or smacking sounds with your lips against the back of your hand or the tips of two fingers. Try to make the squeaks high-pitched and alarmed-sounding.

The terminally self-conscious can make squeaks and alarm calls using an ingenious little device called an Audubon Bird Call. Consisting of a pewter plug that rotates inside a small wooden tube, the caller produces a variety of squeaky noises. In practiced hands, surprisingly realistic imitations of birdsong are possible. Audubon Bird Calls are very inexpensive; they are easily found in nature stores and mail-order catalogs.

Exactly why birds respond to pishing and squeaking is not fully understood. The most likely explanation is that the birds interpret the sounds as the distress call of a bird under attack from a predator and react accordingly. You will notice that the birds you attract by pishing often give their alarm calls in response. Stop pishing once the birds respond — this makes them think they have been successful in chasing off the predator. If you keep pishing, you will cause undue stress to the birds.

Just as birds respond to pishing, they will respond to the sound of an owl's call by attempting to mob the predator. You can easily imitate the whinnying call of an eastern screech owl, or you can purchase an inexpensive, continuous-loop tape of owl calls. A small, battery-powered cassette player will generally play the tape at sufficient volume — it doesn't have to be particularly loud. As with pishing, select a likely spot, turn the tape on, and let it play nonstop for several minutes. If you don't get a response, move on and try the tape somewhere else. If birds do start to come in, turn off the tape. As with pishing, you must let the birds think they have chased the predator away. Move on to another spot a good distance away before you play the tape again. *Never* play an owl tape in the territory of an endangered species.

To attract a particular bird, you could imitate its song. Most people aren't very good at this, however, and prefer to play tape recordings instead. Male territorial birds will respond to imitations or tapes with alacrity because they think another bird has invaded their territory. Tapes in particular must be used with great caution. Simply by imitating a birdsong or playing a tape of it you create unnatural stress for the bird, because you cause it to respond to a nonexistent threat. The more you play the tape, the more stress you cause. Turn off the tape as soon as you get a glimpse of the bird, and don't use it again in that bird's territory. Some refuges now ban the use of tape recordings entirely because overenthusiastic birders have caused nest failures and other problems by playing tapes to excess.

## WEATHER AND SEASON

As a birder, you need to be very aware of the weather, since it has a major impact on the birds you see. The five-second weather summary on the local radio station, or even the longer weather report on the local television station, is no longer sufficient. Learn to read the weather maps in your newspaper. Invest in an inexpensive, battery-powered weather radio. These radios can be tuned only to the local frequency (162.400, 162.475, or 162.550 mHz) used by the National Weather Service. The detailed, accurate, and frequently updated reports from the NWS help you plan your birding so that you may dress appropriately for the weather.

Bird migration is closely tied to weather fronts. In particular, wind can have a powerful effect. Migrants flying north over large bodies of water (the Gulf of Mexico, for example) sometimes encounter bad weather and adverse winds as they near the land. Because the exhausted birds can't fight their way inland against the wind, they come down on the first land they see. In birder parlance, this is called a fallout, and it is a bonanza. The birds are everywhere and are so tired they can hardly move. Fallouts occur with some regularity at predictable places such as Cape May in New Jersey or Point Pelee in Ontario on Lake Erie.

Conversely, migrating birds sometimes encounter unfavorable conditions and adverse winds as they prepare to cross a large body of water. Again, the birds back up, sometimes in spectacularly large numbers, while they wait for conditions to improve.

When bad weather clears up, migrating birds move again. The result can be a wave of birds passing through. One of the most delightful sights for a birder is a wave of colorful warblers in bright spring plumage. The numbers and variety that can be seen in a warbler wave will absolutely astonish you the first time you experience it.

In the autumn, the weather has a significant effect on bird movements. This effect can be seen most profoundly in the case of hawk migration. Because these soaring birds count on thermal currents of warm air, their migration tends to stall when the weather gets cold and rainy. After a few chilly, wet days, a clear, sunny day will bring the hawks down the migration route in large numbers. Cold fronts and low-pressure zones tend to push migrating birds ahead of them; sometimes the passage of large numbers of migrants presages the arrival of significantly colder and nastier weather.

Severe storms or hurricanes can blow birds far from their usual habitat. Offshore storms can drive pelagic (ocean-going) birds close to the shore, where they can be seen with spotting scopes. Shore birds can be driven far inland. A bird found significantly off course in a place where it shouldn't be is called an accidental or a vagrant.

In the spring, birds tend to sing less when the weather is cool and cloudy. Wet, windy weather tends to make birds clam up and disappear as they seek shelter. Sometimes, the passing of a short rain squall can provide you with a birdwatching treat. The birds pop up singing all around you as the sun comes out again.

The easiest birdwatching for beginners probably happens in the spring, when the birds migrate north in large numbers starting as early as March. These birds are wearing their bright breeding plumage and singing loudly, making them easier to identify. In addition, most trees and other plants are just budding out and have not yet developed their full foliage, so the birds are easier to spot.

Birds tend to be much quieter and harder to spot in the summer, but some shorebirds complete their breeding and begin to migrate to their winter territories as early as mid-July. By the end of August, other birds are definitely on the move. Fall migration tends to be more diffuse — there are no warbler waves, for example — but

*The snowy owl* (Nyclea scandiaca) *is generally found well north of the Canadian border, where it feeds on lemmings and other small rodents — one breeding snowy owl can account for 1,300 lemmings in a single year. Occasionally irruptions occur in the winter and the bird is seen in the northern United States. Snowy owls are surprisingly tame and will allow birders to approach quite near. This illustration was done by Alexander Wilson, who wrote and illustrated the first systematic study of American birds, published in nine volumes between 1808 and 1814.*

also more numerous, since the young birds born that year swell the numbers heading south. Birds in autumn are more difficult to identify because, by this time, their breeding plumage has faded. In the winter, there are fewer bird species to see, but they are easier to spot because there is little foliage to get in the way. Put up a bird feeder in the winter and get to know your backyard birds better. Winter also brings the occasional irruption, or large movement of birds into areas beyond their normal range. Irruptions generally occur when a species can no longer find food in its usual range. Irruptive species tend to be birds that depend on food sources that are subject to sudden crashes. When the population of voles and lemmings in the subarctic regions of Canada goes through one of its periodic crashes, for example, raptors such as snowy owls head south in search of food.

## BIRDING ETHICS

You are, of course, an ethical person in your daily life. You also, of course, wish to be an ethical birder. If you apply your usual high ethical standards to your birding, you can't go wrong. If you understand a few specific points, you will never be in doubt about acceptable birding behavior.

All native wild birds, with the exception of rock doves (pigeons), starlings, and house sparrows, are protected by federal, state, and provincial laws. In essence, these laws forbid individuals from harming, killing, capturing, possessing, or otherwise hurting protected birds. The law extends to any parts of birds (feathers), bird nests, and eggs.

The above taboos were first set out on the federal level in the United States and Canada by the Migratory Bird Treaty Act of 1916; they have since been expanded and amended, most notably in the United States by the Endangered Species Preservation Act of 1966.

Theoretically, anyone found in possession of any wild bird or part thereof for any reason is breaking federal law (and probably state or provincial law as well) and can be imprisoned and fined. Aside from licensed hunting, there are some exceptions to the law. Permits are granted for scientific research, banding operations, and other legitimate pursuits. You are permitted to possess a wild bird in an emergency—bringing an injured hawk to a rehabilitation center, for example. It is unlikely, though theoretically possible, that you will be prosecuted for picking up a feather in the woods or bringing home an old nest, but think carefully before you do. Remember that in 1983 Dave Winfield, then an outfielder with the New York Yankees, was arrested after he accidently killed a gull with a warm-up throw during a game in Toronto.

The Endangered Species Preservation Act and its amendments specifically prohibit you not only from possessing a bird but from harassing it in any way, whether deliberately or unintentionally. This means that you are forbidden from doing anything that could cause the bird to change its normal behavior and thus endanger its welfare. You might naively think that no birder would ever harass a bird, particularly an unusual or endangered one, but this sort of behavior occurs among birders with depressing regularity. To cite just one recent example: In August 1991, eared trogons were found nesting in Arizona's Ramsey Canyon. Because this bird has only rarely been seen north of the Mexican border, and because no breeding record existed, birders quite literally overran the area. They trampled vegetation, blasted the birds with taped calls, and otherwise behaved in unacceptable ways, to the point that the trogons abandoned the area and their breeding efforts. They later returned, however, and hatched two chicks. Unfortunately, their breeding had been so delayed by disruptive birders that it was then October; cold weather killed the young.

Using a tape recording to attract birds can be a very effective but also a very controversial technique. Tapes must always be used in an ethical manner that avoids unnecessary stress on the bird. It is obviously unethical to use any tapes at all in the territory of endangered species. It is also obviously unethical to use tapes to excess. Less obviously unethical is the cumulative stress that can occur when different birders play tapes to the same birds. You may not feel you are causing a bird much stress if you briefly play an owl tape to attract it. But what happens when fifteen minutes after you leave, another birder comes along and does the same thing, and another birder after that?

On the other hand, which is preferable: A group of five birders crashing through the undergrowth in pursuit of a bird, or five birders waiting quietly on a trail and calling the bird to them briefly with a tape? Judicious use of a tape recording here is appropriate. Weigh the pros and cons carefully before using a tape. If you have the slightest doubt, don't play it.

Trespassing is an area where situational ethics tend to apply. Birders should avoid trespassing on private property and posted lands. This rule can be flexible, however. Obviously, you should ask permission before entering someone's backyard, farmland, or posted land. On the other hand, say an interesting bird presents itself while you are driving along a deserted road bordered by posted woods. Is it ethical to enter the woods to see the bird? You decide.

If you are birding by permission on private property, be courteous. In particular, stay on the paths and don't trample any vegetation or disturb any animals. Stay out of any fields with crops, including hay, and don't disturb any livestock. Don't enter fields with locked gates; leave other gates as you find them. In residential areas, don't turn up at the crack of dawn or go prowling around in the evening. At best you will be considered a weirdo and a nuisance; at worst you could be mistaken for an intruder.

It is your obligation as a birder to behave in an ethical manner and to make sure others behave properly as well. Read carefully the American Birding Association's code of birding ethics in Appendix A, and take it to heart.

**2**

# Getting Around
# Your Field Guide

· · · · · · · · · · · · · · · · · · · · ·

*T*he presence of a field guide is so well established today among birdwatchers that it is hard to imagine a time when these useful, compact volumes didn't exist. In fact, the birth of the field guide can be dated precisely to 1933, the year Roger Tory Peterson published his revolutionary book, *A Field Guide to the Birds*, illustrated with his own paintings.

Prior to Peterson, ornithologists generally described a bird by listing its characteristics literally from head to toe, giving equal weight to every aspect of the bird's outer physical appearance and usually including a detailed discussion of its internal structure as well. The exhaustive information was of very little help to anyone trying to identify a bird seen fleetingly in the field. And although the detailed and very accurate paintings of John James Audubon were available in cheap, poorly reproduced editions from about 1870 onward, these too were not particularly helpful for field identification.

The genius of Peterson was his brilliant system of identifying the birds by their field marks. Each description and painting points out the few significantly characteristic features of a bird that identify it as that species and no other. The Peterson field mark system was a radical change from all other field guides up to that time. Today, the Peterson system is used by virtually all field guides to the birds and in most guides to other aspects of natural history.

## CHOOSING A FIELD GUIDE

*A Field Guide to the Birds*, or simply Peterson, in eastern and western editions, remains the standard by which all the numerous other field guides now available are judged. It is perhaps the best choice for a beginner simply because it is so readily available, so easy to use, and so familiar to the other birders you will encounter. Other field guides have their advantages, however, and most birders eventually end up owning at least two different volumes.

Aside from Peterson, three other field guides are widely used. *A Guide to Field Identification: Birds of North America*, by Chandler S. Robbins, Bertel Bruun, and Herbert S. Zim, is published by Golden Press; it is often called just the Golden guide and is the guide most often recommended for beginning birders. The remaining two guides are sponsored by major nature organizations: *Field Guide to the Birds of North America* from the National Geographic Society and *The Audubon Society Field Guide to North American Birds*, in eastern and western editions. Beginners may prefer a guide that covers only their region, since it makes identification easier by listing only those birds found there. (Eastern and western North America are divided, somewhat arbitrarily, at the 100th meridian. A better way to think of the division is east and west of the Rockies.)

All the above guides, with the exception of the Audubon Society volume, are organized more or less taxonomically with an illustration near a written description of each bird. (See below for an explanation of taxonomy.) A range map is found either beside the description or at the back of the book. All the guides are indexed; all are fairly compact and will fit easily into a large jacket or pack pocket. A serious drawback to the Audubon Society guide is that it is organized in a very peculiar manner. The front part of the book contains full-color photos of the birds cross-referenced to descriptions found separately in the back part of the book. To confuse matters further, the photographs are organized not taxonomically but by broad categories such as gull-like birds. Within the categories, the photos are organized by the color of the bird. Within the written descriptions, the birds are again organized not taxonomically but by habitat. This sort of arrangement may seem helpful at first, since beginners often note only the most visible colors and have trouble deciding what family a bird belongs to, but it is fundamentally unsound and very unwieldy for field use.

## USING YOUR FIELD GUIDE

The first step in using your field guide is buying it. Any well-stocked bookstore will have at least one of the most popular field guides; decide which you prefer and purchase it. Do not use any musty old field guides you may find tucked away on a shelf of the summer cottage or in a box up in the attic. Ornithology is an ongoing science, and those guides will be out-of-date.

Next, *read* the guide. This does not mean memorize all the descriptions. Rather, read the introduction and instructions on how to use the book. Get a feel for the book's organization and the way the information is presented. Learn how the range maps are set up and what any symbols mean. Browse through the pages and get to know the members of various bird families. Don't spend long periods reading one species description after another — you'll never remember the birds. Instead, spend fifteen minutes or so at a time studying a particular group of birds, or working out which birds you are likely to see in a particular habitat.

At first, finding a bird in your field guide will be a tedious exercise in page-flipping. As you become more familiar with the different bird families, you will be able to narrow the range of possibilities and turn to the most likely section(s) of the field guide quickly. Once you can put a bird into its proper family (more or less), you will probably then be able to identify it specifically. First, try to match the physical appearance of the bird to the illustration. Look for the field marks indicated in the illustration and described in the text. Compare your bird's actions to any behavior and habitat notes mentioned in the guide. Check the range map. If the bird had to be wildly off course to have ended up in your backyard, it's probably not the bird you think it is. Birds do sometimes end up doing uncharacteristic things in the wrong place but, on the whole, they are surprisingly predictable.

After a while, your field guide will fall open at the right pages by itself—one sign that you have passed beyond the beginner phase. Until then, try putting paper clips on the pages you will refer to most on a birding trip. If you're visiting a coastal sanctuary, for example, put clips on the pages covering sandpipers and gulls.

Some useful accessories are sold in birding specialty catalogs and nature stores. Index tabs and stick-on quick indexes for the most common field guides are inexpensive and very helpful. Special waterproof book covers are also available.

Your field guide will be your constant companion both in the field and at home. It will gradually become scribbled in, bent, stained, and torn. You will develop an unreasonable sentimental attachment to it and secretly resent the appearance of a new edition. Worst of all, you will mourn if it is lost. Always write your name, address, and phone number in the front of your field guide. Birders understand how you feel and will make an effort to return a lost guide if they find one.

## THE ART OF OBSERVATION

You love your field guide and you depend on it. Is this a good thing? Maybe not — a field guide can be a crutch that substitutes for close observation. If you go into the field with your guide, you may develop a tendency to stop watching the bird too quickly while you look it up in the guide. You may have the satisfaction of identifying the bird but, in the meantime, you may have missed some interesting behavior or some other birds. It's also quite possible that by simply observing the bird further — getting a better look at its appearance and behavior — you could arrive at an identification without relying on the field guide.

Try leaving your field guide behind or, if this makes you feel too insecure, bring it along and leave it in your pocket. Bring along a small, inexpensive, spiral-bound notebook and a strong rubber band to hold the page down. (Eventually someone will give you a beautiful nature notebook made with exquisite paper and a sewn, hardcover binding. Thank the giver politely and put the notebook to some other use.) Also, bring two inexpensive, retractable ball-point pens with clips (marker pens run on wet paper, pencil points break, and all pens get lost). When you spot an unknown bird, simply watch it carefully. In the case of small, fast-moving birds such as warblers or sparrows, make mental notes of the birds' appearance (this is one of many reasons birders talk to themselves); for larger birds such as ducks or herons, you can often scribble your notes as you watch. Make a sketch, no matter how rough or inept, of any interesting identification features, such as a crest on the head or the shape of the tail. Jot down anything else that might be useful for identifying the bird: an estimate of its size, habitat, and behavior.

Upon returning home, study your notes and try to place the

unidentified birds into the proper families. Next, make your best guess as to what species they are. Only then should you turn to your field guide to verify your identification.

Keeping field notes may be frustrating at first, particularly when you yearn for a life list in three figures. Stick with it. There's no better way to learn the art of observation than by doing it.

Your stained and tattered field notebooks will gradually fill up with observations, directions, phone numbers, restaurant recommendations, and cryptic notes that mean nothing to you three days later. Your notebooks contain your birding life — treasure them.

## BIRD FAMILIES AND BIRD NAMES

The basic concepts of taxonomy — the hierarchical classification of living things by their degree of common characteristics and evolutionary closeness — are crucial to birdwatching. By understanding taxonomy, you understand how the different bird species are related; once you understand the characteristics of a particular bird family, identifying individual species within the family becomes much easier.

### Taxonomy for Beginners

The traditional first question in the game Twenty Questions asks "animal, vegetable, or mineral?" In the broadest taxonomic classification, birds belong to the animal kingdom. Moving down the hierarchy, birds belong to the phylum Chordata, or animals with a hollow dorsal nerve cord. Birds quite literally get into a class of their own — Aves — at the next level down. Here we have the taxonomic definition of a bird: a warm-blooded animal with feathers and wings that lays large, yolky eggs with chalky shells.

The class Aves is divided into about 30 orders, or groups of families. In scientific Latin, orders are indicated by the suffix "-iformes", which means shape. Thus, the various vultures, hawks, and falcons are all members of the order Falconiformes (always capitalized, never italicized). The order Passeriformes is the largest order; it includes most of the birds more loosely referred to as perching birds or songbirds. Orders are fundamental to bird identification — get to know them. Most field guides are organized by order, starting with the most primitive birds (loons) and ending with the most developed (sparrows). In taxonomic terms, primitive simply means oldest in the evolutionary sense.

Each order is divided into several families, indicated by the suffix "-idae". There are about 160 different families altogether. Among the Falconiformes families are the Cathartidae (vultures), the Accipitridae (kites, hawks, eagles, and ospreys), and the Falconidae (caracaras and falcons). If you can classify a bird into its correct family, you have gone a long way toward identifying it. When discussing families within orders, field guides often make some changes in strict taxonomic sequence for the sake of clarity. Again, get to know the various families. You will often hear birders talking about larids, for example. If you have studied your field guide diligently, you will know they are referring to gulls.

Families are subdivided into subfamilies, indicated by the suffix "-inae". Among the family Accipitridae, for instance, are the subfamilies that include kites, accipiters, harriers, buteos, eagles, and ospreys. In some cases, subfamilies are further divided into tribes, indicated by the suffix "-ini". For example, there are six different tribes for ducks.

Next in the sequence comes the genus, or group of similar species. The genus (plural genera) really helps you make sense of the larger families such as warblers, because it combines them into

## BIRD TAXONOMY

All birds, living and extinct, are members of the taxonomic class Aves. The chart below, based on the American Ornithologists Union Check-list of North American Birds, lists the orders, families, and genera of all species of birds known to occur regularly in the continental United States and Canada. Orders are listed in boldface type; families are indented, subfamilies, and tribes within an order are indented further. The common English names are listed first, with the scientific Latin names following in parentheses. Of the approximately 9,000 living bird species, just over 700 are known to occur regularly in North America.

LOONS (Gaviiformes)
  *Loons (Gaviidae)*
GREBES (Podicipediformes)
  *Grebes (Podicipedidae)*
TUBENOSES (Procellariiformes)
  *Albatrosses (Diomedeidae)*
  *Fulmars, shearwaters, petrels*
  *(Procellariidae)*
  *Storm petrels (Hydrobatidae)*
PELICANS AND ALLIES
(Pelecaniformes)
  *Tropicbirds (Phaethontidae)*
  *Gannets and boobies (Sulidae)*
  *Pelicans (Pelecanidae)*
  *Cormorants (Phalacrocoracidae)*
  *Anhingas (Anhingidae)*
  *Frigatebirds (Fregatidae)*
HERONS AND ALLIES (Ciconiiformes)
  *Herons and bitterns (Ardeidae)*
  *Ibises and spoonbills*
  *(Threskiornithidae)*
  *Storks (Ciconiidae)*
FLAMINGOS (Phoenicopteriformes)
  *Flamingos (Phoenicopteridae)*
WATERFOWL (Anseriformes)
  *8 waterfowl tribes (Anatidae)*

*Whistling ducks, swans, geese*
*(Anserinae)*
  *Whistling ducks*
  *(Dendrocygnini)*
  *Swans (Cygnini)*
  *Geese (Anserini)*
*Ducks (Anatinae)*
  *Surface-feeding ducks*
  *(Anatini)*
  *Wood ducks (Cairinini)*
  *Bay ducks (Aythyini)*
  *Sea ducks and mergansers*
  *(Mergini)*
  *Stiff-tailed ducks*
  *(Oxyurini )*

VULTURES, HAWKS, FALCONS
(Falconiformes)
  *American vultures (Cathartidae)*
  *Kites, hawks, eagles, ospreys*
  *(Accipitridae)*
  *Caracaras and falcons (Falconidae)*

GALLINACEOUS BIRDS (Galliformes)
  *Chacalacas (Cracidae)*
  *4 subfamilies of pheasants and allies*
  *(Phasianidae)*

# BIRD TAXONOMY (continues)

Partridges and pheasants
(Phasianinae)
Grouse and ptarmigans
(Tetraoninae)
Turkeys (Meleagridinae )
Quail (Odontophorinae)

CRANES AND ALLIES (Gruiformes)
Rails, gallinules, coots (Rallidae)
Limpkins (Aramidae)
Cranes (Gruidae)

SHOREBIRDS, GULLS, AND ALCIDS
(Charadriiformes)
Plovers (Charadriidae)
Oystercatchers (Haematopodidae)
Stilts and avocets (Recurvirostridae)
Jacanas (Jacanidae )
Sandpipers, turnstones, surfbirds,
phalaropes (Scolopacidae)
4 subfamilies of gulls and allies
(Laridae)
Jaegers and skuas
(Stercorariinae)
Gulls (Larinae)
Terns (Sterninae)
Skimmers (Rhynchopinae)
Alcids (Alcidae)

PIGEONS AND DOVES
(Columbiformes)
Pigeons and doves (Columbidae)

PARROTS (Psittaciformes)
Parrots (Psittacidae)

CUCKOOS, ROADRUNNERS, ANIS
(Cuculiformes)
Cuckoos, roadrunners, anis
(Cuculidae)

OWLS (Strigiformes)
Barn owls (Tytonidae)
All other owls (Strigidae)

GOATSUCKERS (Caprimulgiformes)
Goatsuckers (Caprimulgidae)

SWIFTS AND HUMMINGBIRDS
(Apodiformes)
Swifts (Apodidae)
Hummingbirds (Trochilidae)

TROGONS (TrogoNiformes)
Trogons (Trogonidae )

KINGFISHERS (Coraciiformes)
Kingfishers (Alcedinidae)

WOODPECKERS (Piciformes)
Woodpeckers (Picidae)

PERCHING BIRDS (Passeriformes)
Tyrant flycatchers and becards
(Tyrannidae)
Larks (Alaudidae)
Swallows (Hirundinidae)
Jays, magpies, crows (Corvidae )
Chickadees and titmice (Paridae)
Verdins (Remizidae)
Bushtits (Aegithalidae)
Nuthatches (Sittidae)
Creepers (Certhiidae)
Bulbuls (Pycnonotidae)
Wrens (Troglodytidae)
Dippers (Cinclidae)
Old World warblers, kinglets,
gnatcatchers, thrushes
(Muscicapidae)
Old World warblers, kinglets,
gnatcatchers (Sylviinae)
Old World flycatchers
(Muscicapinae)
Bluebirds, solitaires, other
thrushes (Turdinae)
Wrentits (Timaliinae)
Mockingbirds and thrashers
(Mimidae)

## BIRD TAXONOMY

*Wagtails and pipits (Motacillidae)*
*Waxwings (Bombycillidae)*
*Silky flycatchers (Ptilogonatidae)*
*Shrikes (Laniidae)*
*Starlings (Sturnidae)*
*Vireos (Vireonidae)*
*Wood warblers, tanagers, grosbeaks,*
*sparrows, blackbirds (Emberizidae)*
  *Wood warblers (Parulinae)*
  *Bananaquits (Coerebinae)*
  *Tanagers (Thraupinae)*

*Grosbeaks, tropical buntings,*
*dickcissels (Cardinalinae)*
*Towhees, sparrows, longspurs*
*(Emberizinae)*
*Blackbirds and orioles*
*(Icterinae)*
*Finches (Fringillidae)*
  *Bramblings (Fringillinae)*
  *Cardueline finches*
  *(Carduelinae)*
*Old World sparrows (Passeridae)*

manageable groups of birds that are related in appearance and behavior. A classic example of a genus with closely related birds is *Empidonax*, which contains a number of flycatchers that are almost identical in appearance and present a serious identification challenge. Birds belonging to the same genus are called congeneric.

Finally, the field narrows to the fundamental unit of taxonomy, the species. A bird species is one that is closely related to other members of its genus, but cannot interbreed with them. Every species is assigned a unique, binomial (two-part name) in scientific Latin. These names stay constant even when a bird is known by two or more common names. For example, the American woodcock is also sometimes called a timberdoodle or bogsucker, but scientifically speaking it is always called *Scolopax minor*. The first part of the binomial indicates the genus, always capitalized; the second part indicates the species, always lower case. Species names are always italicized. After the genus has been given in full for the first time, it is often abbreviated to just its first letter (e.g., *S. minor*).

Some species have subspecies. A subspecies is a population of a species that shows some variation, often because of geographic separation, but has not evolved differences sufficient to prevent inter-breeding. Subspecies are sometimes called races. The dark-eyed junco (*Junco hyemalis*) has several subspecies. The most easily observed are the slate-colored race, common throughout Canada and the United States, and the Oregon race, common west of the Rockies. Slate-colored juncos are a uniform gray color on the head, back, and breast; Oregon juncos have a black breast and head, and a rusty back.

## Lumping and Splitting

The basic hierarchical principles of modern taxonomy were laid down by the great Carl Linnaeus in 1735. Since then, advancing scientific knowledge has meant that bird classifications are some-times revised to reflect more accurately the relationships among species — a good reason to use an up-to-date field guide. A classic example was the decision that the "Baltimore" oriole of the east and the "Bullock's" oriole of the west are really the same bird, now listed as the northern oriole with Baltimore and Bullock's as subspecies.

When species are combined, they are said to be "lumped"; when species are divided, they are said to be "split." Needless to say, birders hate it when species are lumped, because it deprives them of a bird on their life list. Fierce controversy can surround taxonomic questions, and recent advances in DNA analysis are sure to add considerable fuel to the flames. The generally accepted arbi-ter of taxonomic questions is the American Ornithologists Union.

## Scientific vs. Common Names

Every bird has a binomial scientific name, as explained above. Every bird also has a widely accepted common or vernacular name that is much easier to remember and pronounce. For example, *Dendroica petechia* is better known by the common name yellow warbler. Colloquial names are nonstandard names applied to a family, genus, or species. Colloquial names tend to be colorful but inexact. For example, goonybird is a colloquial name applied indiscriminately to albatrosses, and whiskey Jack is another name for the gray jay.

How do birds get their names? The scientific name is often descriptive of some aspect of the bird's appearance or behavior. Sometimes it commemorates an individual related to the bird in some way, and sometimes it doesn't seem to bear much relationship to anything. In Linnaeus' time, every educated person knew Latin and Greek and could understand what the scientific name meant, regardless of his or her native language. In our own very different time, few people study Latin and Greek, and the meaning of the scientific name is frequently incomprehensible. For translations, you can do your own detective work with an unabridged dictionary or look the name up in one of the several dictionaries of bird names.

Even if you can remember the scientific name, you may be hesitant about pronouncing it. A good rule of thumb is just to pronounce everything, including every vowel.

Common names, like scientific names, often describe some obvious characteristic of the bird. This is helpful both for remembering the name and for identifying the bird, since the name often points you toward a critical field mark. Common names can sometimes be misleading, however. The red-bellied woodpecker does have a very faintly pink abdomen, but the chief field marks for this bird are its red cap and ladder back. Likewise, the Connecticut warbler is rarely found in that state. Sometimes the common name commemorates an individual. The English naturalist William Swainson (1789–1855) has three birds named in his honor: Swainson's hawk, Swainson's thrush, and Swainson's warbler. The lovely Anna's hummingbird was named in honor of Anna, wife of the Duc de Rivoli, a celebrated beauty in her time (she died at the age of 90 in 1896). All told, there are 77 North American birds named for people. John James Audubon now has just one bird named in his honor: Audubon's shearwater.

# Identifying Birds

$T$he core principle of birdwatching is identifying what you see, but bird identification is probably the most difficult and frustrating aspect of birding for beginners. How can you possibly be expected to know which sparrow you have just seen when, according to the field guide, it could be one of about twenty different species?

The art and science of bird identification consists of observing as many features of the bird's appearance and behavior as possible, combining that information with observations of the season, habitat, and niche in which the bird is seen, and narrowing the range of possibilities down to a single species.

The basic skills of bird identification are not a mystery — they are easily learned by anyone. In fact, you can already identify several birds, and you already possess a good understanding of how to go about identifying birds you don't know. Think about the birds you already can identify. You know some by name: robin, blue jay, mourning dove, crow, mockingbird, and easily twenty or more additional species. You may not know some other birds by species, but you can accurately place them into their family: for example, sparrows, hawks, and gulls.

How do you know all this? Without digressing into a monograph on cognitive psychology, you can recognize some birds because they match the clear mental image you have developed over years of experience — you have been aware of the most familiar birds since childhood. Based on your fundamental knowledge of a few basic birds, you are able to categorize other birds into the appropriate family because you recognize the individual features that are characteristic of the family.

Just as you can recognize a good friend from behind in a crowd of people, or by catching a glimpse of a characteristic gesture, or even by hearing a snatch of his or her laughter, so too can you learn to recognize birds at a glance.

## Basic Identification Steps

Identifying a bird is basically a matter of systematic observation logically applied. Before you can do this, however, you need to be familiar with the concept of bird families (see chapter 2) and with some descriptive terminology. At the front of every field guide is a topographical diagram of a bird that explains the standard terminology used to define the various parts of a bird. Study this diagram carefully and refer to it often.

The first step toward identification is to note the physical appearance of the bird. Next, whenever possible, watch it long enough to note aspects of its behavior. The section below concentrates on physical appearance; an extensive discussion of behavior-watching is in chapter 5.

Once you are focused in on a bird, run through a mental checklist of identifying features. The goal is to note the most obvious field marks and to arrive at a strong overall impression of the bird.

### Color

The beautiful, vivid colors of some birds are often what attracts people to birding. Birds that are all or mostly one bright color are

*The common name of the gray catbird* (Dumetella carolinensis) *gives two important clues to its identification: its overall gray color and its catlike mewing call. The black cap is another distinctive field mark. Alexander Wilson is the artist.*

*Library of Congress*

easy to identify. Their names are easy to remember, since they usually incorporate a reference to the color. Examples include red birds such as cardinals and scarlet tanagers, blue birds such as indigo buntings and bluebirds, and yellow birds such goldfinches. For every bird that is easily identified by its highly visible color, however, there are many more that are basically drab, with only touches of brighter color. In addition, the color of a bird can change with the season. American goldfinches, for instance, are a bright yellow with glossy black wings in summer, but drab khaki with dull black wings in winter.

### Size

You already have a fairly good mental yardstick for noting the size of a bird. Simply compare it to a bird you know well. Is your mystery bird bigger than a sparrow but smaller than a robin? Is it about the size of a chickadee or a rock dove (pigeon)? It's much easier to use a comparison than it is to try to assign an actual numerical measurement. Size can sometimes be deceptive. A bird with fluffed-up feathers in cold weather looks larger than the same bird with sleeked-down feathers in warm weather. Poor lighting conditions also make it difficult to estimate size. Size is also sometimes difficult to estimate through binoculars and spotting scopes. The compression caused by long optics can make a sparrow in the foreground look about the same size as a robin in the background. When estimating size, try to look at the bird both with the naked eye and with optics.

## Shape

The overall shape of a bird is a very important clue. Birders use a variety of words to describe shape: chunky, trim, slender, stocky, plump and sleek. These terms are somewhat subjective because shape can't be defined exactly — it's more of an impression. To get an idea of body shapes, compare the stocky shape of a rock dove with the slimmer body of a mourning dove.

## The bill

If you can look at only one part of a bird, look at the head. Note particularly the shape and size of the bill and try to determine its color (this is harder than it sounds). The bill is an excellent identification clue. Many birds or bird families take their name from the shape or color of the bill: tubenoses, shovelers, crossbills, grosbeaks, yellow-billed cuckoo, spoon-billed ibis, and ringed-bill gull. Bill shapes tend to be very similar within a bird family. Thus,

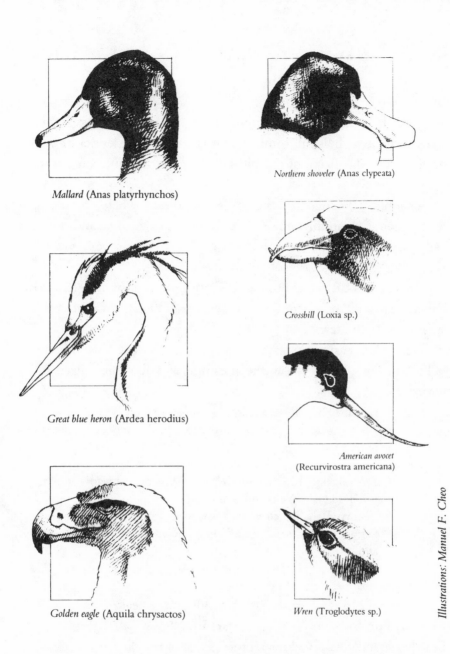

*Mallard* (Anas platyrhynchos)

*Northern shoveler* (Anas clypeata)

*Crossbill* (Loxia sp.)

*Great blue heron* (Ardea herodius)

*American avocet*
(Recurvirostra americana)

*Golden eagle* (Aquila chrysactos)

*Wren* (Troglodytes sp.)

*Illustrations: Manuel F. Cheo*

A bird's bill is an extremely important clue to its identity. Passerines such as wrens generally have small, straight bills adapted to eating insects and seeds. The crossbill feeds by inserting its crossed mandibles into the crevices of pine cones and prying the cones open to reach the seeds inside. Herons have long, powerful bills meant for capturing fish, reptiles, and amphibians in water. The mallard's bill is well-designed for dabbling in shallow water and on the surface. The northern shoveler's bill is adapted to filter feeding. This duck has comb-like plates inside its bill; it feeds by straining small plants and animals from the surface of the water. The long, thin, upward-curving bill of the American avocet is adapted for "swishing" through the sediment below shallow water to stir up food. The beak of the golden eagle is obviously perfectly adapted to tearing.

all geese have broad, round-tipped bills; all warblers have thin, straight, pointed bills; all hummingbirds have long, slender bills. A good look at the shape of the bill can do a lot to point you toward the right family.

The relative length of the bill is important when identifying birds such as sandpipers. For example, the greater and lesser yellowlegs look much alike, but the bill of the lesser yellowlegs is slimmer and much shorter.

Bill color is often hard to see. It's rarely an important field mark when identifying passerines, but it can be significant for other birds such as gulls and terns.

Generally, easily understood adjectives are used to describe bills. You do need to know the meaning of a few specialized bill terms:

- Beveled: the bill has a chisel-like tip (as in woodpeckers);
- Ceres: a leathery "saddle" at the base of the upper mandible (as in many raptors);
- Decurved: the bill curves downward (as in curlews);
- Frontal shield: a flat extension of the bill upward onto the forehead (as in coots and gallinules);
- Recurved: the bill curves upward (as in avocets and some stilts);
- Serrate: the bill has "teeth" along the edges (as in mergansers); and
- Tubenose: external, tubular nostrils on top of the bill (as in albatrosses and shearwaters).

What's the difference between a bill and a beak? There really isn't any but, for some reason, birders usually say bill. Inexplicably, beak is generally reserved for raptors (birds of prey).

## The head

Important field marks are found on the head, as the names of many birds suggest—red-headed woodpecker, for instance. Look particu-

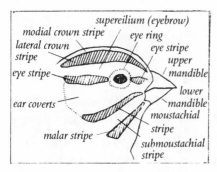

Head markings, as shown here, are important clues for pinning down an identification. Learn the descriptive terms for the various types of markings. In addition, study the detailed drawings in your field guide showing the topography of a bird and the parts of a wing.

Manuel F. Cheo

larly for solid colors, eye rings, eye stripes, crests, and head markings such as stripes, hoods, and masks.

The heads of some birds are a solid color that contrasts with the body color: brown-headed cowbird and yellow-headed blackbird are two self-evident examples.

An eye ring is an area of a contrasting color encircling the eye. Eye rings are sometimes partial or broken, and they are not always easy to see. Sometimes the eye ring can give the bird a big-eyed look, as in the tufted titmouse or ruby-crowned kinglet. An eye stripe or line is a dark line that runs through the eye. A superciliary eye stripe is a dark or light stripe or line that runs above the eye, rather like an eyebrow. The Carolina wren and the chipping sparrow, for example, have conspicuous white eye stripes.

Eye color is sometimes an important field mark, but it is a difficult one to see. Despite its name, the red-eyed vireo is much more easily identified by other field marks such as its monotonously repeated call, its conspicuous white superciliary eye stripe, and its blue-gray cap. The brown thrasher has yellowish eyes, but you should easily be able to identify this bird from other, more obvious field marks.

The color of the lores (the area between the base of the upper mandible and the eyes) is sometimes given as a field mark. If the bird has an eye ring and lores of the same color, and also has a dark eye stripe, it may be described as wearing spectacles. Many vireos have this characteristic field mark.

Head markings such as stripes can easily be seen on birds such as white-crowned sparrows. Colored caps or crowns are good field marks, as in the black-capped chickadee. The chipping sparrow can be spotted at a distance by its rusty cap; this is also a good field mark for the palm warbler. Look for crests or other unusual formations on the head. Crests are seen on such birds as cardinals, tufted titmice, cedar waxwings, and pileated woodpeckers (pileated means crowned or crested). Some ducks have large crests. Good examples are the wood duck and many sea ducks such as buffleheads and goldeneyes. Horned larks have little "horns" on top of the head behind the eyes (these can be hard to see).

*The most obvious field mark for the pileated wood-pecker* (Dryocopus pileatus) *is the large and conspicuous red crest, as shown here in a illustration by Alexander Wilson.*

*Library of Congress*

Face masks are easily seen on cedar waxwings and common yellowthroats. As their name suggests, hoods can be seen on the hooded warbler and hooded oriole, as well as the Connecticut warbler and other birds.

## Throat and breast

If you can get a glimpse of a bird's throat and breast, look for patches of color at the throat and for the presence or absence of stripes and streaks on the breast. Throat patches are conspicuous field marks for such birds as the white-throated sparrow and the ruby-throated hummingbird. Throat patches are also good clues when identifying some warblers: the blackburnian warbler has a distinctive orange throat patch.

Stripes, streaks, and spots on the breast, or the lack thereof, are useful field marks. Many thrushes, for example, have streaked breasts. The presence or absence of streaks is also helpful when identifying sparrows.

## Wings

After getting a good look at the head, move on to the wings and look for bars and patches. These are usually thin lines (bars) or solid patches of a lighter color that run across the folded wings. The presence (or absence) and number of bars and patches are frequently cited as important field marks. Patches on the underwing, such as those of the mockingbird, are easily seen when the bird flies.

Wing stripes are lighter- or darker-colored margins along the wing feathers. These are usually not visible when the wings are

*The black-billed magpie (Pica pica) is easily recognized by its very long tail (only a few North American birds have tails longer than their bodies) and white wing patches. This illustration is by John James Audubon. The Birds of America, Audubon's masterwork, first appeared in 1838.*

*Library of Congress*

*It's hard to distinguish the willet* (Catoptrophorus semipalmatus) *from other marsh sandpipers when they are standing. In flight, however, the willet shows a prominent white wing stripe.*

*VIREO/Frank Schleicher*

folded, but are quite conspicuous when the bird flies. Wing stripes are particularly helpful for identifying shorebirds such as sandpipers and other waders in flight.

Sometimes the wing is a contrasting color, as in the scarlet tanager or blue-winged warbler. The color of the wing lining can also be a field mark, especially when viewing the bird in flight from underneath.

Note the shape and length of the folded wing. Swallows, for example, have long, pointed wings that extend almost to the end of the tail when the bird is perched.

It is important to understand the terminology used to describe bird wings, since you will encounter these terms often. Study the topographical diagram in your field guide to get a firm grasp on the types of feathers — primaries, secondaries, coverts — and the parts of the wing, especially the leading and trailing edges and the wrist.

## Tail

The shape, color, and angle of a bird's tail also provide important identification clues. Note the shape and length of the tail — very long, long, short, stubby, narrow, broad, and so on — and the shape of its end. Tails can be squared-off at the end, notched, pointed, rounded, or deeply forked (as in the barn swallow). The position in which the bird holds its tail is also a clue. Some birds, such as wrens, hold their tails cocked up at a jaunty angle; others routinely hold their tails down almost vertically. Some birds, including many flycatchers, "wag" their tails up and down as they perch.

*The long tail, streaked breast, and rich cinnamon color of the brown thrasher (Toxostoma rufum) make it fairly easy to identify. Beginners often confuse this bird with the wood thrush (Hylocichla mustelina), but the wood thrush has rounded breast spots and a much shorter tail. This illustration is by Alexander Wilson.*

*Library of Congress*

## Feet and legs

The color, length, and structure of a bird's feet and legs are sometimes very difficult to see. The feet and legs are not that important for identifying most birds, especially the passerines. However, leg color is helpful for identifying gulls and terns and some shorebirds. Leg length is a good field mark for some wading birds such as sandpipers.

One of the more baffling bird names you will encounter is the semipalmated sandpiper, one of the most abundant shorebirds. The name describes the bird's feet. You need to know some descriptive foot terms:

- Lobed: flat, paddle-shaped toes (as in grebes);
- Palmated: webbed between the front three toes (as in ducks, gulls, loons);
- Semipalmated: partial webbing between the front toes;
- Totipalmate: webbed between all four toes (as in cormorants and pelicans); and
- Zygodactylic: having two toes facing forward and two facing backward (as in woodpeckers).

You won't get many opportunities to use these terms, since you probably won't get a very close look at the feet of a wading or swimming bird. Learn the vocabulary so you can sound reasonably intelligent—especially if you can work zygodactylic into the conversation—but don't count on foot structure as a field mark for identification purposes.

## Flight

Just when you get your binoculars focused on that brown bird in the branches, off it flies. Don't give up—the flight itself can help you identify the bird. Some field marks are visible only when the

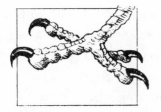

Woodpecker

Ptarmigan

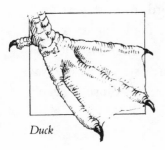

Duck

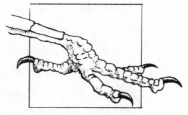

Passerine

Raptor

Grebe

It's hard to get a good look at a bird's feet, but if you do you'll have some additional clues toward indentification. All birds have four toes. Webbed feet are found on swimming birds such as ducks and geese. Some birds that swim and walk on land about equally, such as coots and grebes, have lobed toes. Birds of prey (raptors) have powerful, clawed toes that are highly separated. Passerines have four separate toes, generally with three facing foreward and one facing backward; these feet are designed for perching. Woodpeckers are zygodactylic: they have two toes facing forward and two facing backward. The ptarmigan has "snowshoes" of feathers on its feet to help it walk on the suface of snow.

Illustrations: Manuel F. Cheo

bird flies. Indeed, the appearance of the bird in flight is practically the only way to identify some of the look-alike shorebirds. A more familiar example is the dark-eyed junco, which is easily spotted by the flashing of its white outer tail feathers as it takes flight.

The way the bird flies is also a clue. Hummingbirds hover, fly backward, and even fly upside-down. Dabbling ducks take off from the water in one jump, while diving ducks have to patter along the surface building up speed before they can take off. Hawks soar; swallows fly with elegant strength; mockingbirds fly with very slow wing beats; and woodpeckers have an undulating flight, folding their wings against their bodies after several wing beats. With experience, you will be able to identify many birds simply by the way they fly. This is a skill worth cultivating, if only because it deeply impresses nonbirders.

## Posture

The way a bird stands, perches, and moves is another helpful clue. Some birds perch with an upright posture, while others perch more horizontally. Note also the way the bird walks. Does it hop on both feet? Does it walk on alternate feet?

## Identification complications

Seasonal plumage changes can seriously complicate life for beginning birders. A bird's most vivid and recognizable plumage occurs during the breeding season. When that period is over, the bird's distinctive colors and patterns can gradually fade. This is exemplified by the warblers, whose bright spring colors and clear markings become drab and indistinguishable by autumn. Roger Tory Peterson coined the very apt phrase "confusing fall warblers" to describe the phenomenon.

Shorebird identification is also complicated by seasonal plumage changes. Gull identification is further complicated by seasonal changes and by the plumage changes immature birds go through before reaching adulthood.

Identification challenges of this sort are extremely interesting for advanced birders and extremely frustrating for beginners. If you can't identify the species, just let it go as an unidentified warbler, sandpiper, or gull.

## Making the Identification

The illustrations in your field guide present the birds in static profile wearing idealized plumage. Surprisingly often, birds actually do present themselves in profile and hold still long enough for you to get a good look. Often enough, however, they are far less obliging. As discussed elsewhere, you must apply all your birding techniques to getting a glimpse of a good field mark or a distinctive piece of behavior.

Sometimes all you need is the one definitive field mark that excludes all other possibilities. If you see a small, bright yellow bird with black wings, it can only be an American goldfinch.

It is more likely that you will have to narrow down the possibilities by a process of elimination. Start by trying to place the bird in its proper family. The good field mark, along with your overall impression of other characteristics, should at least get you into the right section of your field guide. Once you are looking at the descriptions of the most likely family, you can try to pin your bird down specifically. Check the range maps. Birds do stray from where they should be, but the odds are against it. Check the habitat.

Again, birds are sometimes found outside their usual habitat, but not often.

To take a real-life example, suppose you are birding in a marshy area—Jamaica Bay in New York City—and you notice a small, brownish bird moving restlessly among the phragmites. As the bird briefly pops up into an open space, you distinctly see that its short tail is cocked upward; you get the impression that the bird has a white eye stripe, but it vanishes again before you can be sure. What bird have you seen?

The upcocked tail tells you that the bird is some sort of wren. But which of the nine possible wrens is it? By looking at the range maps, you can immediately eliminate those that are not found on the East Coast. This removes Bewick's wren, the cactus wren, the rock wren, and the canyon wren from consideration, leaving you with only five possibilities. By considering the habitat, you can further eliminate the house wren, winter wren, and Carolina wren. Now you are left with just two possibilities: sedge wren or marsh wren. Habitat and the general impression that the bird has a white eye stripe point you directly at marsh wren.

The first time you go through this process, you may not find the bird, probably because you are looking in the wrong family. It's very easy to confuse a female rose-breasted grosbeak with a member of the sparrow family, for example, and even very experienced birdwatchers can't tell some of the flycatchers apart. Even if you get close on the first try, it could take you a long time to decide on the final identification. The whole laborious business can start to make you feel terribly inept. You will despair of ever achieving the immediate identifications that other birders do with such nonchalant ease. Stay with it. The day will come when, catching sight of an interesting bird, to your own surprise you automatically identify it correctly.

*All wrens have characteristic short, upcocked tails. A white eyebrow line over the eye and a solid rusty cap distinguish the marsh wren (Cistothorus paluatria) from other wrens.*

VIREO/Allan D. Cruickshank

Work at your identifications, but don't get hung up on identifying every bird you see, especially if it means that you're not having any fun. Remember the words of Walt Whitman, an enthusiastic if somewhat indiscriminate nature-lover: "You must not know too much, or be too precise or scientific about birds and trees and flowers...; a certain free margin, and even vagueness... helps your enjoyment of these things."

# Birding by Ear

$W$hen it comes to finding and identifying birds, sound can be as important as appearance. Learning to recognize bird sounds will increase your enjoyment of birding enormously.

Birds make a variety of sounds with a variety of purposes. The most recognizable bird sounds are the lovely notes warbled by songbirds, but virtually all birds (swans and vultures are among the rare exceptions) have songs of a sort and make other sounds called vocalizations. All bird vocalizations are produced by the syrinx, an organ located in the trachea just above the branching of the bronchi leading to the lungs. As a rule, the more developed the syrinx, the more complex the sounds it can produce. Songbirds generally have highly developed syrinxes and thus produce the most complex song. Interestingly, because the song is produced entirely within the syrinx, many birds can sing with their mouths full or even closed.

Every songbird species has a distinctly different song, full of rich harmonics. Birds outside the songbird family also produce distinctly different calls and other sounds that are an aid to identifying the species and to determining where the bird is and what it is doing. For example, it is visually difficult to tell the difference between a lesser and greater yellowlegs unless two birds are near each other for a size comparison. However, the voices of the two species are quite different and easily distinguished.

## SONGS

Birdsong or vocalization, whether complex or simple, is a male function, designed primarily to define territory. Another significant function is to attract a mate; this accomplished, the male sings to his mate to strengthen the pair bond. (With rare exceptions and despite all the inaccurate poetry about nightingales, female birds do not sing.) The same functions of birdsong are accomplished in other ways by some other birds. Woodpeckers, for example, define their territories and attract females by drumming on resonant surfaces such as trees (and sometimes houses or even cars).

Birdsong reaches its peak in the early mornings of spring, when male birds are vying for territory and advertising for mates. A bird walk through woods and fields at this time of year is a delightful cacophony of sounds. Singing drops off noticeably once the birds get organized, with all the borders staked out and females spoken for, but it continues at a reduced level into the breeding season. By midsummer, birdsong almost ceases.

Singing birds in the spring are easy to find—just follow the sound to the tree branch or shrub that contains the singer. The birds will generally be found perched prominently on the tops of the trees, at the ends of the branches, or on top of other vegetation or telephone poles, the better to project their voices, keep an eye on the competition, and spot any interested females. Singing birds generally adopt erect postures, with the head back and the beak wide open. They thoughtfully repeat their songs loudly over and over from the same place, allowing birders to home in.

As part of claiming their territory, some birds such as cardinals will counter-sing or duet with nearby rivals. When this occurs, first one, then the other bird sings alternately. Once you realize that at least two birds are involved, you can separate the sounds and go in search of one or the other.

Locating a singing bird can be difficult. The first step is simply to stand still and listen intently, concentrating on only the bird you are tracking. This can be surprisingly difficult, especially for city dwellers who are accustomed to ignoring all the undifferentiated noise constantly around them. It can also be difficult for older birders, who may no longer be able to hear very quiet song or the high notes. Try turning your head slowly from side to side while listening; you should hear the bird more loudly toward one side or the other. All members of a group should listen carefully and slowly point to where they think the sound is coming from. Theoretically, this should yield an accurate consensus. There's a good chance, of course, that just when you think you have located the bird it will fly away. Stick with it. Generally, a territorial bird won't fly far and you still have a good chance of getting a look at it.

In general, birds sing the most in the early morning and toward dusk. Some birds, including some flycatchers and swallows, sing special dawn songs just before day breaks. The function of dawn songs, aside from their beauty, is unclear, unless they are an incentive to birdwatchers to get up early.

## OTHER SOUNDS

Particularly among songbirds, a distinction is generally made between songs and other sounds. Male, female, and young birds all produce a wide range of calls and other sounds that help the birder locate and identify them. Generally, a bird's repertory of sounds falls into several convenient categories: alarm calls, contact calls, flocking calls, feeding calls, begging calls, flight calls, aggressive calls, and non-vocal sounds such as woodpecker drumming. Unfortunately, these sounds are often not as well-defined as songs, making it difficult sometimes to determine which bird is making the sound and why.

Especially to inexperienced birders, the various chips and chirps made by different birds sound much alike. With practice, you will gradually begin to recognize the more obvious differences among species. Some differences are so slight as to be virtually undetectable; in such cases, even experienced birders need other clues to identify the bird.

What a particular bird sound means must often be determined from the context. For example, the contact call (the sound members of a pair make to keep in touch with each other) of the white-breasted nuthatch is often described as *yank* or *yank-yank*. The same call, given louder and more frequently, is an alarm call.

## LEARNING BIRD SOUNDS

A unique sort of vocabulary is used by the authors of field guides and other written descriptions to transcribe bird sounds. When reading descriptions, the easiest to remember and imagine are those that are onomatopoeic, or imitative of the actual sound. A classic example is the *chicka-dee-dee-dee* call of the black-capped chickadee, which sounds exactly as it is written. Other songs and calls are not as easy. Songs are often described as melodious, clear, whistled and slurred. Calls may be described as a harsh chatter, buzzy trill, or rattle call. Songs and calls are also often transliterated as a burry *teeooo*, raspy *chur*, or a simple *chip*, *tseep*, or even *ik* or *chjjj*. Even worse from a beginner's standpoint are descriptions that compare one bird's song with another's, since you are likely to be unfamiliar with both. And what exactly is the difference between sounds that are buzzy, burry, and raspy? Are birds that go *chjjj* also found on Klingon?

Beginning birders can take comfort in the knowledge that the experts disagree among themselves about how to describe and transliterate bird sounds. For example, Roger Tory Peterson renders the song of the Acadian flycatcher as "a sharp explosive *pit-see*," while other guides render it variously as *PEET-sah*, *peet-suh*, and *flee-see*; the usual mnemonic is *Pizza*!

No amount of puzzling over the correct pronunciation of *tsickajwee-jwee* (tufted titmouse) or *woika woika* (red-bellied wood-pecker) can ever substitute for hearing the real thing. Ideally, you will locate and identify a new bird, hear it vocalize, and forever re-member the sound and associate it with a clear mental image of the bird. The association can be complicated by some variables. Many songbirds sing individual variations on the basic song, and individ-ual birds sing variations of their variations. Some birds do good imitations of other birds — blue jays often imitate the screams of hawks, and the mockingbird's song consists of nothing but imita-tions of other birds. In addition, the basic song can vary by geogra-phy. In effect, birds develop dialects. This is often noted even by casual birdwatchers when they hear song sparrows in other parts of the country. Finally, birds make lots of simple call noises that sound a lot like those of other birds. Remember that even the most experienced birders usually know only the usual territorial song and most common call sounds for a species. When all you hear are as-sorted *chips*, you might as well give up on an aural identification. Use the sounds to locate the bird for a visual identification instead.

## SONOGRAMS

Some field guides provide a sonogram, or visual representation of the song, by the description of the bird. At first glance, sonograms seem arcane and impenetrable. They are in fact more useful once you are familiar with the bird's song, but they provide helpful information even if you're not, once you know how to read them. The vertical axis of a sonogram indicates the pitch (frequency) of the song, as measured in hertz (Hz) or kilohertz (kHz — one kilohertz is the equivalent of 1,000 hertz). For a reference point, middle C on a piano is at 0.262 kHz; the highest C on a piano is at 4.186 kHz. Most birdsong takes place between 2 and 6 kHz (2,000 to 6,000 hertz), with much of it above 4 kHz. Older adults may no longer be able to hear birdsong at pitches above 6 kHz. The horizontal axis of a sonogram indicates the duration of the song; most sonograms are given in 2.5-second segments. The louder the sound, the darker the marks. Thus, the hieroglyphic dark markings within the sonogram indicate the pitch, duration, and loudness of the various notes in the song.

By looking at a sonogram, you can get a good idea of the general nature of a particular bird's song. The higher the frequency in kHz, the more high-pitched the sound. The more clearly defined the frequency, the purer the sound and the fewer harmonic overtones it has. Clear whistles appear as thin bands within a narrow frequency range; buzzy trills are thick bands within a wide frequency range. Repeated elements can easily be seen.

A good way to begin understanding sonograms is to study that of the wood thrush. This common woodland bird has an easily learned, distinctive, and very beautiful song that begins with high, flute-like notes and ends in a soft trill. The range in kHz is from just below 2 up to nearly 8; the song lasts for about 2.5 seconds and is generally repeated ten to twenty times in a minute. Look at the sonogram while listening to the song to see how the sound relates to the visual representation. The loud, clear notes in the first part of the song are shown by thin, dark bands, while the trill in the last part is shown by a much thicker band that has two parts: a heavy band ranging from about 5 kHz to nearly 8 kHz and a series of vertical bands underneath it ranging from 2 to about 4.5 kHz that are the harmonic tones of the trill. Pay careful attention to the duration of the song and how often it is repeated — these are very helpful identification clues.

## MNEMONICS

Once you've actually heard a song, a mnemonic that attempts to capture its rhythm and cadence helps you remember and identify the song the next time. A mnemonic by definition is memorable. Once you've learned a mnemonic like "When I see one I shall seize one and I'll squeeze it 'till it SQUIRTS!" for the warbling vireo, it's hard to forget. Simpler examples of birdsong mnemonics include "Potato chip, potato chip" for the American goldfinch and "Cheerily, cheerily, cheer up" for the American robin. There's disagreement about some mnemonics. The white-throated sparrow says "Poor Sam Peabody, Peabody, Peabody" if you're a Yankee and "Sweet sweet Canada, Canada, Canada" if you're not. (Roger Tory Peterson steers clear of controversy by describing the song of this bird as "several clear pensive whistles.") Birds don't necessarily start their songs at the "beginning." They sometimes begin in the middle of a phrase, or add a note or two before getting down to the real song. The American goldfinch, for example, often says "Chip, potato chip, potato chip."

## BIRDSONG RECORDINGS

The next best thing to seeing and hearing a singing bird is listening to recordings on cassette and, increasingly, on CD.

Older recordings such as those assembled by Donald Borror briefly present the most characteristic songs or sounds of the birds

*A Western meadowlark* (Sturnella neglecta) *sings from a perch on a fencepost. Many male birds sing from an elevated, exposed perch to indicate their territorial boundaries. Meadowlarks are members of the Emberizidae family, which also includes blackbirds and orioles.*
Bill Bevington

*Many adult birds continue to feed their young until the fledglings are nearly full grown. Note that the young house sparrow here droops its wings in a begging gesture.*
John Heidecker

*Feather care takes up a lot of a bird's time. Here a tricolored heron (Egrotta tricolor)* preens *under its wing. The white underparts are a good field mark for distinguishing this heron from the little blue heron (Egretta caerulea)*
Tim Daniel

*Because of its popularity as a cartoon character, the greater roadrunner (Geococcyx californianus) is a well-known bird. But cartoons—and sometimes even field guide illustrations—don't always prepare you to identify the real thing.*
Big Bend Natural History Association

*The American avocet (Recurvirostra americana) feeds by sweeping its upcurved bill along the surface of shallow water to capture insects and larvae. The extremely long legs and unusual feeding strategy of this bird make it easy to identify.*
R.E. Barber

*A killdeer* (Charadrius vociferous) *feigns a broken wing in a distraction display meant to draw a predator away from the nest.*
Photo/Nats

*Diving ducks such as this common goldeneye* (Bucephala clangula) *must "run" or "patter" along the surface of the water to generate enough lift to take off.*
Jeffrey Rich

*An evening grosbeak* (Coccothraustes verspertinus) *preens a flight feather. Birds "nibble" at their long wing and tail feathers to smooth them for efficient flight.*
Pat Looi

*In a very typical pose, a juvenile burrowing owl* (Athene cunicularia) *twists its head around for a better view of the terrain. These little owls are often seen in prairie dog towns; they are also often spotted at airports in Florida and across the Southwest.*
Eileen Oram

Four black-headed gulls are commonly found in North America. To distinguish this bird from the other black-headed gulls, consider the location. This photo was taken on the East Coast, thus eliminating Franklin's gull and the sabine gull and leaving only the laughing gull and Bonaparte's gull as possibilities. This bird obligingly poses on a piling and clearly shows the orange bill and dark legs of the laughing gull (Larus atricilla).
Michael Baytoff

Two snowy egrets (Egretta thula) perform an energetic mating dance. Note the bright yellow feet.
Photo/Nats

*Chips fly as a red-headed woodpecker (Melanerpes erythrocephalus) excavates a nest hole. Note the zygodactylic feet — two toes facing forward, two toes facing backward — characteristic of woodpeckers. Note also how the bird braces itself using its stiff tail feathers.*
Richard Day

in strict taxonomic order, with a human voice stating the bird name before the sound. You can also get recordings that are keyed to the most common field guides. Taxonomic recordings are useful as reference tools — for verifying your identification of a particular bird — but they are not very helpful for learning the sounds to begin with. More recently, excellent programs that take a teaching approach, including explanatory narrations and accompanying booklets, have become available. These recordings cover the common species not taxonomically but holistically. Some group the birds by similar or related sounds, using the compare and contrast method. Others focus on a particular group of birds such as owls or warblers, or on birds of a particular habitat such as common backyard birds or shorebirds, or on birds of a region. These tapes present many or all of the sounds a particular species makes, not just its song or most common sound. Two that are recommended are *Birding by Ear* (eastern and western versions), by Richard Walton and Robert Lawson, and *Know Your Bird Sounds* (in two volumes), by Lang Elliott. The widest selection of bird tapes (and videos) is found in the American Birding Association's sales catalog; the Crow's Nest Birding Shop catalog also has a good selection.

Bird sounds are often very similar to other sounds in nature. The indignant squeak of a startled chipmunk, for example, can sound very much like the noise made by a startled towhee. Since both noises will come from the underbrush in a wooded area, you could easily start looking for a bird that isn't there or decide not to look for one that is. Alternatively, you might decide that the trilling noise coming from an overgrown field is an insect, when in fact it is coming from the aptly named grasshopper sparrow. The more inexperienced you are, the harder it is to distinguish between bird sounds and those made by insects, frogs, squirrels, and other creatures. Recordings of the sounds of a particular habitat such as a wetlands region can help you learn the differences.

Many birders listen to tapes while driving, but you should probably be alone or in the company of a fellow enthusiast if you do this. These are not the sort of tapes your carpool will necessarily appreciate, especially if you like to practice your bird imitations while listening. Dozing pets will often awaken when you put on the recording; they may then proceed to bark at or look for the "bird." This can be deafening when dogs are passengers in the car. Fortunately, all cats and all but the most obtuse dogs quickly realize that there is no bird and that it is safe to go back to sleep.

For many people, the best approach to bird tapes is to listen for only a short period of just ten minutes or so, but to listen often. Some people have a natural ability—sometimes but not always correlated with musical talent—for learning bird sounds quickly. Most beginners need a fair amount of repetition.

## VIDEOTAPES

Videotapes featuring birds are useful and enjoyable tools for learning to identify birds both visually and aurally. Birding videos fall into three categories. Nature videos tend to be recordings of television nature shows that are wholly, partially, or incidentally about birds; these are usually very well produced and informative. Hunting videos are instructional tapes that by definition focus on ducks, geese, turkeys, and other game birds. If you stifle your initial revulsion at the idea of shooting a bird, you will learn a lot about the behavior of the species in question. You will also learn a lot about how to see that species, since there is little difference between sneaking up on a bird to shoot it and sneaking up on it to see it.

Finally, a number of well-made videos about basic birding, the birds of a particular area, bird families, and other similar topics have become available. Most of these are produced specifically with birders in mind and provide useful information, like a range map, that is usually missing from videos oriented more toward entertainment values.

Nature videos are easily available from any good video rental store; they can also often be borrowed very inexpensively from your public library. Hunting videos are more likely to be found in video stores in rural areas. Birding videos, unfortunately, are on the expensive side. They are also in relatively low demand and aren't usually carried by video rental stores. However, you may be able to persuade your local library to purchase some bird videos; your local bird club may also have videos that members can borrow or that are shown at meetings.

# Bird Behavior

· · · · · · · · · · · · · · · · · ·

*W*hen you observe bird behavior, you realize that there is no such thing as an uninteresting bird. Behavior-watching adds depth and insight to your birding, as well as giving you valuable clues that help you identify and appreciate the bird.

## FEEDING BEHAVIOR

Birds spend a lot of time looking for food, which means that bird-watchers spend a lot time watching them do it. How a bird finds its food, what it eats, and how it consumes it are valuable identification clues. A bird's feeding strategy can help you identify it by family and by species.

Overall, birds consume an amazing variety of food, much of it unpalatable by human standards. Earthworms, carrion, spiders, tadpoles, poison ivy berries, and grass are just some of the foods eaten by various birds. Some birds, such as snail kites, have very specific dietary preferences, while others, such as crows, will eat almost anything.

To find their food, birds employ a number of different feeding strategies. Many strategies are common or even unique to a particular bird family; however, many birds employ more than one feeding strategy, or employ a particular strategy only when a particular food is abundant. By observing the feeding strategy of a mystery bird, you can probably place it into the correct family and then move on to identify the species.

## Pecking

Probably the most familiar feeding behavior is pecking, where the bird searches on the ground for food, picking up seeds, insects, and other food. This is very common behavior for passerines such as sparrows, juncos, finches, and mourning doves, and for larger gallinaceous (chicken-like) birds such as ruffed grouse, bobwhite, and wild turkey.

Often the bird scratches at the ground or uses both feet to stir up the leaf litter and reveal insects, seeds, and nuts. Pecking and leaf-tossing can be seen easily in your backyard under the bird feeder by watching the juncos, house sparrows, and white-throated sparrows. You will also often see fox sparrows and rufous-sided towhees doing this. On a bird walk, listen for the rustling noises these birds make as they forage. Pecking birds tend to be found on or near the ground, often in open areas such as fields, roadsides, yards, and open woods.

## Probing

Of all the familiar bird feeding behaviors, probing may be the most familiar of all, since it is performed by that most familiar of birds, the American robin. When you watch a robin take a few steps across the lawn, pause, cock its head, and then suddenly thrust its bill down into the ground and come up with a worm, you are seeing the probing strategy in action. (Despite the appearance of listening, robins actually cock their heads to focus the fovea—the most sensitive part of the eye—on the ground to spot the movement of the worm. In general, birds don't have particularly acute hearing.)

Numerous shorebirds, including dowitchers, godwits, sandpipers, and others probe the sand and mud for food. Dowitchers and godwits probe with a characteristic rapid "sewing-machine" movement. Woodcocks and snipe also probe for food.

Probing also refers to poking into and under bark and other cracks and crevices to find food. Among the common backyard birds, brown creepers and nuthatches are champion probers.

## Chiseling

Woodpeckers are the clearest example of chiseling as a feeding strategy. Chiseling works in two ways: First, the pounding on a tree trunk makes a hole and exposes the insects, insect eggs, and larvae; second, the pounding disturbs other insects and makes them come to the surface, where they are promptly eaten. The noise made by a

*The pileated is the largest North American woodpecker. In this illustration by Alexander Wilson, a pileated woodpecker strips loose bark off a dead branch to search for insects and larvae underneath. Note the long, oval-shaped holes chiseled into the tree — these are characteristic of the pileated woodpecker.*

*Library of Congress*

foraging woodpecker is easily heard in the woods, but can be hard to pinpoint because it is irregular. Look for large trees with dead portions, dead or dying trees, or trees with old broken branches and stubs; these tend to have insects boring into them and are attractive to woodpeckers. Even if you don't actually see the woodpecker, you can see signs of its activity: fresh holes in the tree and wood chips on the ground. Look at the size and shape of the hole. Pileated woodpeckers make large, oblong holes; hairy and downy woodpeckers make smaller, rounded holes.

Sapsuckers use another form of chiseling to drill rows of small holes, or wells, in the bark of trees. The sapsuckers use their brush-like tongue to lick up the sap that accumulates. If you find a tree with sapsucker wells, sit down and watch it for a while. Other birds, including hummingbirds, warblers, and vireos, may visit the spot to feed on the nectar and the insects it attracts.

Woodpeckers are often unfairly accused of killing trees. There is some slight truth to this, because sapsuckers (small North American woodpeckers) occasionally drill their holes so efficiently that they girdle the tree and it eventually dies. Usually, however, the tree is already dying from insect infestation, which is what attracts the woodpeckers to begin with.

## Perch-gleaning

The strategy of searching for insects and other small prey such as spiders or insect eggs while perched on a branch or twig is called perch-gleaning. Warblers, which eat insects almost exclusively, use this strategy frequently as they move through the woods and underbrush. Perch-gleaning birds usually move rapidly and energetically in their search for food. They will land on a branch, search the immediate area, and then flit on to another nearby spot. This activity is one way to distinguish between warblers and other, slower-moving denizens of the treetops such as vireos.

You can easily observe perch-gleaning by watching chickadees and titmice forage. These energetic, acrobatic little birds search rapidly among bark, leaves, and other foliage, sometimes hanging upside down, and then move quickly to another spot. Perch-gleaning behavior is seen even when these birds take seeds from a feeder: they seize the seeds and dart away to hammer them open and eat them elsewhere.

### Plucking and pruning

Many birds eat seeds and fruits that they pluck or glean directly from the vegetation. For example, cedar waxwings love to eat berries, wild cherries, and grapes. A small flock of these birds will descend on a wild cherry tree and eat their fill, sometimes politely passing the fruits to each other. Goldfinches land on the seed heads of wild grasses and glean the seeds, along with any insects they find. Other birds that eat seeds and fruit in this manner include purple finches, house finches, and blue jays. An excellent way to observe this feeding strategy is to stake out a food source such as a patch of ripe berries and wait to see which birds come to exploit it.

Pruning is a more specialized feeding strategy. Birds such as grosbeaks and ruffed grouse nip off the tender, nutritious buds of trees and plants.

### Hawking

This feeding approach is easily seen in the behavior of members of the flycatcher family. The bird perches quietly, often wagging its tail slowly up and down, then suddenly darts out, seizes a passing insect, and returns to its original perch or another one nearby. Phoebes and other flycatchers often find telephone wires or branches on the edges of open areas or ponds to be convenient hawking sites. Kingbirds prefer bushes in open fields. Some fly-catchers, including the willow, least, and Acadian, dart out to capture insects that are on leaves or branches, a form of hawking sometimes called sally gleaning. You might also spot a red-eyed vireo sally gleaning. Birds that are not part of the flycatcher family also hawk for insects. The list includes cedar waxwings and some woodpeckers.

## On the wing

Some insect-eating birds such as swallows, swifts, and nighthawks capture their prey in flight. The graceful gyrations of swallows as they pursue insects on the wing are a birder's delight. An interesting feature of all these birds is their wide gape — that is, the soft, fleshy tissue around the corners of the mouth. The wide gape in effect makes their mouths bigger, allowing the birds to engulf their insect prey easily.

Barn swallows are very common and easy to watch; other swallows are also quite common. Look for them perched on telephone wires and TV antennas, especially in areas near open fields and lakes.

## Raptor feeding

Birds of prey generally capture their meals by seizing them after a pursuit (accipiters such as Cooper's hawks, for example) or by pouncing on them from above (owls, eagles, and buteos such as red-tailed hawks, for example). Peregrines and other falcons capture their prey by stooping — diving down on the prey at great speed. Kestrels and rough-legged hawks hover hunt, beating their wings rapidly to hold themselves stationary in the air before pouncing.

The short, rounded wings and long tails of the accipiters are superb adaptations for chasing small birds through wooded areas. Watching a sharp-shinned hawk pursue a flicker while twisting among the tree trunks with incredible speed and agility is a sight that will take your breath away the first time you see it. If you visit a hawkwatching locale during the fall or spring migration, it is a sight you have a reasonably good chance of seeing. Accipiters sometimes pick off birds at feeders. This is perfectly natural; don't interfere.

Red-tailed hawks and the other buteos such as the broad-winged hawk are heavier and larger than the accipiters. Their prey is usually larger as well: rodents and rabbits are preferred. Buteos soar in high, lazy circles, watching the ground for unwary prey. They then drop down rapidly in a steep dive and land, feet first, on the prey. Red-tailed hawks are the most common and widespread hawk in North America. Although there is a fair amount of variation, red-tails are basically easy to spot and identify as they circle; look for the characteristic rusty-colored tail. If a red-tail wants a closer look at a possible meal, it may face into the wind and hold itself motionless, an action known as kiting for its resemblance to a kite on a string. Red-tailed hawks often drift out of sight before you get a chance to see them kite or dive.

The hover-hunting and pouncing behavior of kestrels can be seen without difficulty. These handsome little hawks are quite common. Look for them on telephone wires and poles, fence posts, and other lookout perches near open areas such as fields or even highway median strips. When a kestrel spots something to eat, such as a small rodent or a grasshopper, it may pounce immediately. Alternatively, kestrels cruise their territory, hover when they spot potential prey, and then pounce.

The chances of your seeing one of nature's most dramatic moments — a peregrine falcon stooping on its prey — are much better than they once were. Thanks to successful release programs across North America, these endangered birds now live comfortably atop tall buildings and bridges in cities such as Cincinnati, Calgary, Baltimore, Los Angeles, New York, San Diego, Winnipeg, and Pittsburgh. You may also be fortunate enough to see a peregrine fly past a hawkwatching site during the fall migration. If you are extremely fortunate and have fast reflexes, you may see it stoop.

### Scavenging

Vultures, crows, and gulls are nature's clean-up crew. These birds spot dead animals from the air, then land and feed on them. Vultures eat almost nothing but carrion; crows and gulls are much more flexible. Turkey vultures and black vultures are often seen soaring slowly over their large territories. You can usually watch them turn their heads slowly from side to side, looking for carcasses as they soar. If you notice several vultures making low, tight circles, chances are something large and dead, like a deer, is below them somewhere. You may also startle a vulture dining on roadkill by the side of a quiet country road.

### Plunging

When you are birdwatching in a marshy area, you may see a dark, chunky shape hover briefly over some water, then suddenly drop down into it head-first. Before the splash is over, the bird flies back up, usually with a small fish in its mouth, and lands on an over-hanging branch. You have just seen a belted kingfisher plunging for prey. Plunging birds dive all the way into the water from the air or from a perch. Other plunging birds include pelicans, ospreys, and terns—all fish-eaters. White pelicans are quite common along the West and Gulf coasts; brown pelicans are less common but perhaps more familiar, especially to visitors to Florida, since they often hang around fishing piers looking for handouts. Despite their awkward-ness on land, pelicans are marvelous flyers. You have a pretty good chance of seeing them feed if you visit an ocean coast or take a sea-going boat trip.

That terns generally plunge into the water in pursuit of food on or just below the surface is one good way to distinguish them from gulls. As with pelicans, your best chance of seeing this behavior is to look in coastal areas or offshore.

## Grazing

Geese, including the very familiar Canada goose, graze on veg-etation on the land or water's edge by pulling it up or biting it off. Any large bird that seems to be nibbling the ground is a goose.

## Dabbling

One of birding's more endearing moments is watching a dabbling duck such as a mallard up-end itself and waggle its rump while feeding underwater. More practically, feeding behavior is a good way to narrow down the identity of an unknown duck. Dabbling or surface-feeding ducks are usually found in shallow areas of salt- and freshwater marshes, or on other shallow water such as small ponds. This is because they feed by eating vegetable matter on or

VIREO/Allan D. Cruickshank

VIREO/ F. Schleicher

*One way to sort out the birds floating in the water is by their profiles. Ducks float high in the water, showing all of their wings and tails, as in this photo of an American wigeon (Anas americana). Loons and grebes appear to be much lower in the water, often seeming partially submerged, as in this photo of a red-necked grebe (Podiceps grisigena).*

*An anhinga* (Anhinga anhinga) *in a very characteristic pose and place: holding its wings out to dry on a dock.*

just below the surface. Mallards, black ducks, pintails, blue-winged teal, and other dabbling ducks often share their habitat, especially during migration periods, with bay ducks such as redheads and canvasbacks and sea ducks such as buffleheads and common goldeneyes. The differences in feeding behavior can help you sort out the different species.

## Diving

Diving birds float on the water's surface and then submerge completely in pursuit of prey or vegetable matter. Bay ducks and sea ducks commonly dive for their food. If you are watching a duck and it tips itself up and disappears under water, it is a diving duck. Other diving birds include grebes, cormorants, and anhingas. Grebes dive by silently sinking out of sight, a slightly unnerving thing to watch.

As a rule, swimming and diving birds are well adapted to a watery life, with feathers that shed water. Cormorants and anhingas, however, are not waterproof. After diving for food, they must spread their wings out to dry in the sun. Cormorants and anhingas are thus very easy to spot on land. In coastal wetlands, look for large, blackish birds perched on pilings, tree stubs, and the like, with their wings held half-open. Double-crested cormorants are widespread, even inland; anhingas are found in freshwater swampy areas in Florida and along the Gulf Coast.

### Stalking

Many members of the heron family stand in or wade through shallow water in search of live prey, a strategy known as stalking. A stalking great blue heron clarifies the Zen-like connection between stillness and motion. The bird stands for long moments in shallow water, motionless but deeply intent, then darts with lightning speed and unerring accuracy to snatch its prey from the water. Great blue herons are the largest herons in North America. They are common and easy to watch in both salt- and freshwater wetlands. These herons are surprisingly tolerant of humans. They will often let you get quite close and will sometimes even accept handouts.

Canopy feeding is a refinement of the stalking strategy. Some herons, including reddish egrets, snowy egrets, and Louisiana herons, stand in shallow water with their wings spread up and outward. Exactly why the birds do this is not really understood. Many researchers believe that the outspread wings act as a sunshade, blocking glare on the water and giving the bird a better view of possible prey.

## Sediment stirring

Shorebirds and wading birds that feed on small organisms sometimes stir up the sediment in shallow water to find their prey. Herons, egrets, and storks all do this. A good example is the way the snowy egret delicately dabbles shallow water with its yellow feet as it flies past. Another approach to sediment stirring is followed by phalaropes which spin in circles like tops in shallow water to stir up food with their lobed feet.

## Surface feeding

Gulls and many other sea birds such as petrels and shearwaters obtain their food by plucking it from the water's surface. Indeed, the name shearwater comes from the way these birds fly just along the very edge of waves; sometimes the wingtips of shearwaters can be seen actually dipping into the water as the birds fly. With consummate skill, these birds pluck fish, shrimp, and other food from the water. You can easily watch a herring gull surface feed by tossing any sort of food — a french fry, for instance — into the water.

Black skimmers are perhaps the ultimate surface feeders. These intriguing birds fly just above the surface of coastal bays with the long lower mandible of their large red bills shearing through the water. In no other North American bird is the lower mandible longer than the upper; no other bird behaves like a black skimmer. Look for flocks of skimmers flying in parallel lines along calm water, especially at dawn and dusk.

## Piracy

If you still have any lingering ideas about innocence in nature, piracy as a feeding strategy will dispel them. Some birds habitually obtain their food by stealing it from other birds. Many gulls are occasional pirates, chasing other birds with food until they drop it. If you watch enough gulls, you will see this happen fairly often. The most skillful pirate is the appropriately named parasitic jaeger. This offshore bird feeds almost exclusively by chasing terns and forcing them to give up their prey. You have a reasonably good chance of seeing this behavior if you take a pelagic birding trip.

## Hoarding

Some birds, notably some members of the woodpecker, nuthatch, and jay families, hoard or cache food. Acorn woodpeckers cram huge numbers of acorns into holes excavated in trees (and also telephone poles). More than 50,000 acorns have been counted in one hoard, or granary. Similar behavior is seen in the Lewis' woodpecker. The hoarding behavior of the Clark's nutcracker has been extensively studied. This bird stores acorns, nuts, and other food in a variety of places, including in the ground and under leaf litter. It has an amazing ability to find its hoarded food again. If nuthatches come to your backyard feeder, you may see one wedge a sunflower seed under a piece of loose bark or into a crevice in a tree, or you may see it rediscover food stored earlier.

## Feeding flocks

Anyone with a backyard birdfeeder is familiar with feeding flocks. Particularly in winter, birds such as chickadees, titmice, and downy woodpeckers form small, mixed flocks and forage together for food. Why is this advantageous? Mixed flocks are more efficient. By flocking together, the birds increase the chances of coming across a good food source (like your feeder), of avoiding areas that have already been picked over, and of overwhelming the defenses of any individual bird that might object to their presence. And because each species in the flock has a slightly different feeding strategy but essentially the same diet, competition for food is reduced relative to the level that would prevail in a same-species flock of the same size. Always look carefully at any flock of feeding birds. You may well see several species.

### Commensal feeding

Also called secondary feeding, commensal feeding occurs when one species finds food as a result of another's activity. As mentioned above, a good example of this is the way hummingbirds and warblers sometimes feed at the holes made by sapsuckers. Among shorebirds, commensal feeding can be seen in "beaters" and "attendants." For example, cormorants often act as beater birds by stirring up prey; they are followed by attendant birds such as snowy egrets that snatch up the prey dislodged by the cormorants' feeding activity. Similarly, cattle egrets follow cows and other livestock, catching the insects these animals stir up with their hooves. Human activity can also be the beater. Birds such as robins and gulls follow tractors in fields to feed on the earthworms and other prey turned up by the plow. Commensal feeding is actually fairly common. Once you know what to look for, you will see it often.

## FLIGHT BEHAVIOR

Birds in flight fill us with longing and admiration. This aspect of birdwatching is endlessly fascinating in itself, and is also a big help in answering identification questions.

## How birds fly

Basically, a bird's wing is an airfoil. As the bird moves horizontally through the air by flapping its wings, the leading edge of the wing "splits" the air. This makes the air flowing over the top of the wing travel a longer distance than the air flowing under the bottom of the wing. The air flowing over the top of the wing moves faster and thus exerts less pressure (Bernoulli's law, from introductory physics class). The higher pressure underneath the wing forces it up, providing lift. When lift is equal to or greater than the bird's weight, the bird flies. (The aerodynamics of bird flight are extremely interesting, but far too complex for this book. For an excellent study of the subject, see *Bird Flight*, by G. Rueppell, and the works of Colin Pennycuick.)

For observing bird flight, you need to understand the structure of a bird's wing and the function of the primary and secondary feathers. Study the diagram in the front of your field guide to learn about the wing. Primary feathers are the outermost feathers — the ones toward the outer end of the wing. These are the feathers most responsible for forward thrust and lift. The secondary feathers on the inner part of the wing form a smooth airfoil.

## Wing shape

Although wing shapes vary enormously among different species, all basically function to provide lift for flight. The shape of the wing can help you identify the bird, at least by family. For birds in flight, look for the overall shape of the wing. Does it taper to a point? Is it

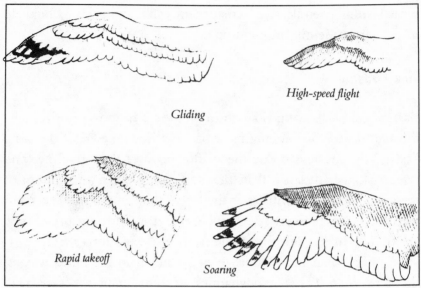

*High-speed flight*

*Gliding*

*Rapid takeoff*

*Soaring*

Manuel F. Cheo

*The shape of a bird's wings (technically, the aspect ratio) indicates the way the bird flies. Gulls, albatrosses, and similar birds have long narrow wings with a high aspect ratio designed for high-speed gliding (upper left). The short, rounded wings of birds such as quail and grouse have a low aspect ratio that allows fast takeoffs and quick maneuverability (bottom left). Many birds found in open areas — terns, swallows, kestrels, for example — have wings with pointed tips. These wings are very efficient with little drag, allowing rapid flight in open areas but relatively little maneuverability (upper right). Wings designed for soaring (lower right) have slots between the primary feathers at the wingtips. Air is forced upward through the slots, improving lift and helping birds such as red-tailed hawks and turkey vultures to soar for hours with little effort.*

rounded? Is it narrow or broad? Are the wings long or short in comparison to the body? Can you see slots between the primary feathers at the tip of the wing? Generally, passerines and woodpeckers have wings that taper to a point—as in swallows, for example. Gallinaceous birds such as wild turkeys have shorter, rounded wings. Herons have broad, rounded wings, while gulls have long, narrow, pointy wings. Crows and vultures have easily visible wing slots.

## Flight styles

If you watch different birds in flight, you will soon realize that they fly in different ways. The things to look for here are the bird's body position in flight, the speed of the flight, how the bird moves its wings, and the nature of the flight. Study the illustrations and flight silhouettes in your field guide. Look at the position of the head relative to the wings: Is it above the wings or level with them? Swans, for instance, fly with their necks extended, while loons fly with their heads lower than their bodies. Are the bird's feet visible beyond the tail? Next, get an impression of the way the bird flies. Consider its speed and the nature of the wingbeats. Rapid flight is a good field clue, especially when applied relatively — common goldeneyes, for example, are very fast fliers, faster than most other sea ducks. Generally, wingbeats are described in field guides by their amplitude: either shallow or deep (if the guide doesn't mention them, assume that they are not especially noticeable). Green herons, for instance, fly rapidly with deep wingbeats; geese fly with deep, powerful wingbeats. The flight pattern and rhythm is also a clue. Woodpeckers and finches have an undulating flight pattern, as if they were on a roller coaster; snipe fly in zigzags. Observe the rhythm and wingbeat frequency of the flight. Does the bird flap its wings continuously? Does it flap several times and then glide? If so, count the flaps and try to time the length of the glide. Noting the rhythm of the flight is particularly helpful for identifying flying hawks.

## Takeoff

The way a bird takes off helps you determine its identity. This is particularly helpful for ducks and other waterfowl. Dabbling ducks such as mallards and wood ducks have a larger wing area to weight ratio (wing loading) and can take off by springing directly from the water's surface. Diving ducks such as canvasbacks and buffleheads have smaller wings relative to their weight and need a running start to get airborne. They head into the wind and patter over the surface to take off. Other waterfowl such as grebes, swans, and geese also need a running start. This is why often only dabblers are found on small bodies of water — they can take off without needing a runway.

## Flight sounds

Flying birds sometimes make characteristic sounds. To take an obvious example, hummingbirds' wings make a loud humming or whirring sound. Mourning doves make a whistling noise with their wings. Owls, on the other hand, fly silently. (Wing noises as part of courtship displays are discussed below.) Many birds call in flight. A few, such as the lark bunting, sing in flight as well.

## Flocking flight

The V formation of Canada geese in flight is well known to almost everyone. Look carefully at any V formation: it is probably geese, but it could be ducks, swans, cormorants, or glossy ibis. Listen while you watch. Canada geese are extremely noisy in flight, honking constantly, while the other birds are quieter; cormorants are silent. Migrating ducks and swans often fly in lines instead of Vs.

## Feather care

Birds have different kinds of feathers. Contour feathers are what most people think of when feathers come to mind. These feathers have a hollow central shaft with vanes on either side. The vanes are made up of individual filaments that hook together with tiny barbs. Contour feathers give birds their shape, color, and markings; specialized contour feathers on the wings allow the birds to fly. Down feathers are shorter than contour feathers and have no barbs to hold the filaments together. The down feathers are found underneath the contour feathers. The fluffy down feathers trap air near the bird's skin, where it is warmed by body heat. Some birds, such as pigeons, herons, and hawks, have specialized down feathers that disintegrate into powder as they grow.

Birds use their bills to preen: that is, to clean, rearrange, and oil their feathers. Preening also smoothes the feathers and closes any gaps. You will often see a bird "nibble" at its feathers to fasten the tiny barbs of the vane filaments together. Birds use their bills to take oil from the preen gland located on their rumps and spread it over their feathers to keep them waterproof and flexible. Birds that produce powder down distribute it over their feathers to aid in waterproofing.

Passerine birds often take baths, splashing in shallow water. The primary purpose of bathing is to rid the feathers of old preen oil. To rid themselves of ectoparasites such as mites, ticks, fleas, and lice, small birds such as wrens and sparrows take dust baths. These birds find areas of loose, dry soil and "bathe" in them, behaving as if the soil were water.

Anting is an intriguing passerine bird behavior. You may sometimes see a bird pick up an ant and rub it over its body; birds also sometimes squat down over anthills and let the ants swarm over their bodies. Exactly why the birds do this is not fully understood. Current thinking is that the ants secrete substances that kill fungus on feathers.

As feathers wear out, they loosen in their sockets; new feathers growing in from within the socket push the old feather out, a process called molting. Most birds molt once or twice a year over a period of one to two months before and after the breeding season. Hawks molt much more slowly, taking as long as two years to replace all their feathers. This often allows birders to identify individual resident birds by their conspicuously missing tail feathers.

## DISPLAY BEHAVIOR

Display behavior consists of predictable actions by birds in response to specific situations. Display behavior can be divided roughly into two categories: territorial and courtship. In these circumstances, a bird will display its plumage or some other conspicuous characteristic and engage in a series of stylized actions, often accompanied by specific vocalizations. (Bird sounds are discussed in chapter 4 as well.)

Observing display behavior is a very good way to identify birds, both by the behavior itself and by the good look at field marks the behavior offers. Head crests, for instance, are usually very visible during territorial encounters.

### Territorial displays

A territorial display is a predictable action by a bird used to define its territory or to defend it in response to an incursion. Among the passerines, a bird's territory is generally all or part of its home range: the area in which it courts, breeds, feeds, and carries on all its other usual activities. Among gulls and other birds that nest in dense colonies, territory is sometimes as small as the area just around the nest. No matter what the territory's size, birds actively defend it against intruders of the same species. (Remember, different species can occupy the same habitat if they use different niches.) Thus, a lot of territorial behavior is virtually indistinguishable from aggressive behavior. At the same time, because establishing and defending a territory are crucial to attracting a mate, the displays and actions used in territorial displays are often very similar or even identical to those used in courtship displays and in defending the nest. Often you must be aware of the context of the behavior in order to assess it correctly. Territorial behavior generally is strongest in the spring and early summer as the birds compete for mates and then raise their young. It tends to become less intense after this.

Many birds, especially the passerines, use song or other sound (woodpecker drumming, for instance) to define the boundaries of their territories. Like song, finding and defending a territory is a male function almost exclusively, so much so that the males of some species, such as the red-winged blackbird, migrate north several weeks sooner than the females to get started on establishing territories.

Aggressive territorial behavior is often signaled by the bird's posture. An annoyed Canada goose, for example, stretches its neck out horizontally, holds its head down low, and hisses. Many passerines also use a horizontal posture, with the head forward and the wings slightly spread, during aggressive encounters.

Another form of territorial behavior is the display of conspicuous plumage or other features. Red-winged blackbirds, for example, perch to sing in a conspicuous spot such as the top of a cattail and flash their vivid red shoulder patches. In aggressive encounters, meadowlarks flash the white outer feathers of their wings and tail; eastern kingbirds fan their tails to display the white margin. Tufted titmice, when threatened, raise their head crests. Many birds puff out their feathers, raise their crests, fan their tails, spread their wings, and otherwise do things that make their bodies look larger and more threatening. When they do this, you can usually get a good look at the markings and colors of the plumage.

Flight displays are sometimes used to indicate territory. Red-winged blackbirds sometimes glide slowly from one perch to another around the boundaries of their territory, flashing their shoulder epaulets the entire time. Other birds such as mockingbirds sometimes fly out from a perch on the border of the territory, make a short loop, and come back to the perch. Hummingbirds can be surprisingly aggressive in defense of their territory, swooping repeatedly in loops to drive off other birds and predators. Killdeer make circling flights over their territory while giving the characteristic killdeer call. Shorebirds use flight displays quite often, since they can be seen easily in the open terrain. When observing a flight display, look for the same things as when observing flight in general. In addition, look for the height and direction of the flight, listen for any calls during the flight, and watch for plumage displays. Don't stop watching after the bird lands. The display often continues, with strutting, wing motions, and other behavior.

Other interesting, easily observed forms of territorial behavior include bill-waving or tilting, head-bobbing, and bowing. You can readily see this sort of behavior and most other forms of territorial and aggressive behavior by observing the birds at your feeder or the pigeons in a park. You can also easily see appeasement behavior here as birds respond to threatening behavior by retreating, often with their heads lowered and turned away.

If an intruding bird doesn't get the message from the display behavior, the defending bird may escalate its defenses, to the point of chasing or actually attacking the intruder. These encounters are fairly common. Feathers may fly and there may be a lot of noise, but serious harm is rare. Sometimes, backyard birds will mistake their own reflection in a window for the presence of an invader. Since the "invader" doesn't respond to the usual territorial displays, the bird ends up attacking the reflection.

## Courtship displays

Once a female bird is attracted to the male's territory, he begins to court her with special display behavior. Courtship displays can take many forms, some quite spectacular or elaborate.

One form of courtship display is breeding (sometimes called nuptial) plumage. This is the colorful, sometimes quite elaborate plumage a male bird develops during the breeding season. The special plumes that a male great egret grows to attract a female are so spectacular that the bird was hunted nearly to extinction for them in the late 1800s.

Flight, often accompanied by sounds or vocalizations, is an important component of courtship displays for many birds. Many raptors perform spectacular aerobatics in the air. Birds such as meadowlarks, found in open areas that lack high perches, hover in the air and sing their songs. Hummingbirds swoop back and forth in large arcs while making chirping noises. These birds position themselves so that the sunlight strikes their iridescent plumage and shows the colors off to best advantage. Woodcocks gather at dusk in open areas called leks. The females watch as the males soar high into the air and then plummet downward, giving a characteristic *peent* call as they fall.

Dancing is part of the courtship ritual for many shorebirds, cranes, and gallinaceous birds such as prairie chickens. Dancing can involve a number of stylized actions, including jumping, wing movements, bill pointing, "curtsies," presenting food or nesting materials, and similar behavior. Prairie chickens, sharp-tailed grouse, and sage grouse perform strutting and stamping motions on leks while making "booming" noises with the air sacs on their necks or chests.

Waterbirds such as ducks often chase each other as part of their courtship behavior. Ducks also do a sort of dance, splashing in the water and performing exaggerated head and neck motions.

An excellent way to see stylized courtship behavior is to watch colonial birds such as great blue herons. These large, angular birds build bulky platform nests of sticks in trees in wetland areas; they are quite tolerant of human observation. As part of its courtship behavior, the male bird brings sticks to the nest and presents them to female with stylized motions that include bowing, stamping, and croaking or hissing vocalizations. He may also make short, circular flights from the nest. Many scientists believe that modern birds are direct descendants of the dinosaurs. Watching and hearing the activity at a heronry at dusk, it is almost possible to imagine yourself back in the Jurassic period.

Among most passerines, courtship behavior is generally less extravagant. Males usually display to the female with characteristic behavior, which could include chasing, bowing, strutting, spreading the wings and tail, and presenting nesting materials. A few common birds, such as cardinals, perform courtship feeding. The female cardinal stands next to the male and begs for food by shivering her wings and making a special call. The male responds by gently placing a seed in her bill. One of the best ways to observe typical courtship behavior is to watch park pigeons. These birds display quite obviously throughout the year.

## NESTING AND PARENTAL BEHAVIOR

As with other aspects of bird life, nesting and parental behavior vary greatly from species to species, ranging from practically nonexistent to very involved.

Birders need to be particularly careful when watching nesting and parental behavior. Birds that are disturbed or harassed before they have laid their eggs may desert the nesting site. If this happens, the birds may then have to nest in a less desirable place or skip breeding altogether. Never watch a nest site for more than a few minutes if your presence is disturbing the birds. In heavily birded areas, it might be a good idea not to watch nest sites at all. Your few minutes, combined with the few minutes of every other birder in the area, might be too much for the birds. Be extremely careful not to disturb any vegetation around a nest. By breaking a branch off to get a better view for yourself, you might also reveal the nest to a predator such as a raccoon or snake.

If you see birds carrying nesting materials (feathers, twigs, mud, grass, or plant fibers) or insects to feed the young, try following them to find the nest. You may not have much luck. Many, though not all, nesting birds are very stealthy, often quietly taking circuitous routes to well-concealed nests. Blue jays, ordinarily raucous and very visible, practically disappear during their nesting season. Many birds exhibit caution displays as they approach their nests, especially if they know predators or humans are watching. Look for birds that are behaving nervously by sitting very erect, flicking their wings and tails, wiping their bills, and performing other fidgety actions. This behavior tells you that the bird knows you are there. If you feel you are preventing the bird from tending to its nest, leave.

*Two immature bald eagles* (Haliaeetus leucocephalus) *await the arrival of parent birds bringing food in this photo. Bald eagles are brown mottled with white until the fourth year, when they develop the characteristic white head. Bald eagle nests are made of sticks in the tops of large trees. Because a mated pair used the site for years and continually adds to it, the nest can eventually weigh a ton or more.*

Taking the habitat approach to nesting sites is often more productive. Look in places where the bird is likely to nest, and listen for the sounds of contact calls from the adults and peeps from the chicks. Phoebes commonly nest on sheltered ledges; house finches are fond of ornamental evergreens. Look for small round holes in the trunks of large, dead trees to find cavity-nesters such as woodpeckers and chickadees. Also listen for the sound of woodpecker drumming, since they often do this near the nest site. Don't try to

peer through the leaves and branches of bushes and dense vegetation. Crouch down, put your head under the bush at ground
level, and look up. Despite all your maneuvering, you may not see
the nest. As the leaves fall in the autumn, you will see a surprising
number of nests that you never noticed in the spring and summer,
even at places you visited often.

## Distraction displays

While walking through a field with your dog in the late spring, you
come across an injured killdeer that flutters along, dragging one
wing pathetically and giving pitiful chirps. Your dog gives chase and
you follow to prevent mayhem, only to see the bird suddenly fly off
normally. The killdeer has just successfully lured you away from its
nest with a distraction display. Feigning injury is a common distraction display among ground-nesting birds such as spotted sandpipers, killdeer, and many shorebirds and waterfowl.

Another form of distraction display is "rodent running." Here
the bird distracts a potential predator such as a coyote from the nest
by running off in a rodent-like manner. Rodent running is seen
mostly in rails and shorebirds.

## MIGRATION BEHAVIOR

For centuries, bird migration was deeply mysterious. Where did the
birds go when they disappeared for months on end? Until well into
the nineteenth century, some observers believed that swallows
hibernated at the bottom of ponds, like frogs. Today we know a lot
more about bird migration, but many unanswered questions still
remain. Whatever the reasons for it, bird migration provides fabu-
lous birdwatching.

## Migration periods

Most migratory birds head south in September and October and north in April and May. These are very approximate times, however, since some of the birds that breed in the Arctic have started south again by the end of July. When birds return north from their wintering areas in Central and South America, they arrive in North America starting in March. Obviously, these birds will arrive in Canada several weeks later.

Many passerines migrate at night, landing at daybreak to feed and rest. Raptors migrate by day to take advantage of thermals.

## Flyways

Migrating birds follow four main paths, or flyways, in both directions: the Atlantic coast, the Pacific coast, the Mississippi River, and the central states. At points along these routes, natural features such as mountains can concentrate the birds, but generally the migration routes are across broad fronts that are sometimes many miles wide. Migration patterns along the Pacific coast are somewhat less well defined, but by positioning yourself in any flyway during migration, you will see a lot of birds. Most birding hot spots are located along flyways.

## Migrant traps

Migrant traps are areas of suitable bird habitat surrounded by areas of unsuitable habitat—a waterhole in a desert, for example. A well-known migrant trap is Central Park in New York City. In the spring, hungry, tired birds spot this oasis of green in a desert of concrete and come in for a landing. Well over two hundred species have been seen in the park. Migrant traps are found everywhere, although you may need local knowledge to find them—another good reason to join your local bird club.

# Seeing More Birds

*I*f you've mastered the basic principles of bird identification and have a good start on your life list, you're ready to see more birds by identifying some of the trickier species and venturing farther afield.

## WARBLERS

Watching warblers is a great aesthetic pleasure and a great identification headache. For beginners, part of the problem is simply that there are so many different warbler species. As with other aspects of birding, approach warblers systematically and the confusion will lessen somewhat.

Warblers (or wood warblers, to distinguish them from Old World warblers, family Sylviidae) are found only in the New World. There are about fifty members of the Parulidae family, divided into sixteen genera, found north of the Rio Grande. Some, such as the yellow warbler, are widespread; others, such as Townsend's warbler, have somewhat restricted ranges; a few, such as the Colima warbler, have very restricted ranges. All warblers are migratory; many spend the winter in the tropics.

Warbler identification is easiest in the spring, when the males are in their colorful and distinctive breeding plumage and sing often. Warblers in the spring tend to travel in small, mixed flocks.

Warblers are often first spotted by their size and behavior.

These small, active birds are most often seen darting around looking for insects in overgrown areas having low trees, brushy undergrowth, and water. Once you've spotted a warbler, try to get a good look at its head — warblers can be identified by their heads alone. Don't bother looking at the bill, since you already know that the bird has a long, thin one. Instead, note the colors and markings. Next, look for wing bars. Many field guides divide warblers into two categories: with and without wing bars. Next, look for colors on the throat and rump.

Note where the bird is within the habitat. Warblers search for food at various levels within the woods, a phenomenon known as layering, or stratigraphic preference. In a classic ornithological study, the distinguished ecologist Robert MacArthur discovered that five different warblers apparently sharing the same niche actually occupied different layers of the habitat. MacArthur studied the foraging habits in conifers of the Cape May, yellow-rumped, black-throated green, bay-breasted, and Blackburnian warblers. Each warbler foraged for insects in a separate part of the tree; in addition, each warbler foraged in a somewhat different manner.

In practical terms, layering means that if you see where in the woods the bird is, you have an important clue to its identity. High-level warblers are found toward the tops of the tallest trees; mid-level warblers are found in the bottom two-thirds of tall trees and the tops of small trees and undergrowth. Low-level warblers are found below eye level down to the ground. Your field guide will often, but not always, mention a warbler's stratigraphic preference.

When watching warblers, the action is often very fast. Don't take the time to look up each bird in your field guide as you see it — you could easily miss other birds in the meantime. As it is, in the time it takes you to get your binocs on the bird, it may well flit away.

Listen carefully for songs. Warblers, despite their name, don't really warble, but each species does have a distinctive, usually high-pitched, song. If you can identify the song, you have identified the bird. Some of the most common warbler songs, such as the ovenbird, are found on most birdsong tapes and are easy to learn.

Warblers in autumn are even more of a challenge. By the time warblers are ready to head south again, their colorful breeding plumage and distinctive patterns have faded, although they are still dimly visible; immature birds have not yet reached adult plumage and are also drably colored. Roger Tory Peterson coined the apt phrase "confusing fall warblers" to describe these birds. Every field guide has a separate section showing autumn warblers, but it's not much help. If you can't identify a confusing fall warbler, don't worry about it — you are very far from alone.

## SHOREBIRDS

Shorebirds are hard for everyone to identify, not just for beginners. You may not believe this as your field trip leader quickly and confidently identifies four different sandpipers standing on a mud flat while you are still trying to get a handle on just one, but even the leader was a beginner once.

To watch shorebirds, use a spotting scope. Your binoculars will never give you the detail you need to see the birds well and attempt an identification.

Focus on standing birds. Shorebirds in flight are very hard to identify. Why try, when most of the birds are standing within easy scoping range? Home in on a small group of birds and look carefully at each one. Chances are they are mostly all the same species, with a few individuals of different species mixed in with the crowd. Work on identifying the most numerous species; you can then work out the oddballs by process of elimination. Be patient and systematic. The shorebirds aren't going anywhere in particular, so take your time.

To begin placing a shorebird into its proper family, look first at its overall shape. Note its silhouette, bill shape, and bill length. Look especially for birds with very long legs, very long bills, or a plump, roundish shape. Before you head to the wetlands, study the shorebird silhouettes found in your field guide. With a little homework and some practice, you will soon be able to distinguish the families. This doesn't necessarily get you too far, since most of the birds you see will be one of the eight common plovers (family Charadriidae) or one of the thirty-eight common sandpipers (family Scolopacidae). The sandpiper family includes the easily re-

5cm _____
10cm _____
15cm _____
20cm _____
25cm _____

*Different birds can share the same habitat if they use different feeding strategies. As shown in this drawing, various shorebird species have bills of differing lengths, ranging from the very short bills of the plover family to the extremely long bills of the curlews. All these birds feed on worms, crustaceans, and other small creatures found at different depths within the same shoreline habitat.*

*Illustrations: Manuel F. Cheo*

cognized curlews and godwits, but also includes the "peeps," six very similar small sandpipers. Of the other common shorebirds, the two oystercatchers (family Haematopodidae) are easily recognized, as are the American avocet and black-necked stilt (family Recurvirostridae).

Next, consider the habitat. Shorebirds have distinct preferences: some are found on sandy beaches, others on coastal mud flats, and others in freshwater marshes. Your field guide will usually mention a species' preferred habitat.

After you have sorted the birds into basic categories, you can try to go further. Here's where it gets really hard. The biggest problem is plumage, since a shorebird could be wearing one of several types. Males and females of most shorebirds look much alike. Your field guide depicts adult birds in full summer breeding plumage (also called basic plumage) and full winter plumage (also called alternate or, rarely, eclipse plumage). Unfortunately, the birds are often in transitional stages between seasonal plumages. In addition, young shorebirds could be in juvenile plumage (first plumage after the downy stage), first winter plumage (not the same as adult winter plumage), or first summer plumage (not the same as adult breeding plumage). To make it all even more confusing, shorebirds all tend toward the same tans, grays, browns, and buffs in cryptic patterns. When watching shorebirds, try to identify them by shape and behavior, not plumage. If you are interested in shorebirds, lots of good identification hints are found in the pages of advanced guides and specialized books.

## GULLS AND TERNS

The good news here is that it is easy to distinguish between gulls and terns (all members of the Laridae family), based on all the usual field marks: shape, tail (terns have forked tails), bill, color, and feeding behavior.

Beyond that, identification gets a little trickier. The terns are complicated, but the field marks and distribution patterns are fairly clear. Study your field guide to learn the marks, and then practice.

For gulls, you will need to apply all your basic birding ID skills along with the ability to remember as many as five to nine different plumages for each species. Gull identification is too complex to deal with here, particularly since it is the author's biggest weakness as a birder. Guides to advanced birding discuss the topic exhaustively.

Beginning birders should particularly note that there is no such bird as a seagull.

## PELAGIC BIRDING

If you want to fill in all those blanks at the start of your checklist, you will have to go on a pelagic birding trip. Pelagic means ocean-going; to see these birds, you must be ocean-going yourself, preferably on a chartered boat with a lot of like-minded birders. Many birding clubs and organizations arrange pelagic trips. They can be a little expensive, especially if you live inland and must travel to meet the boat, but they are definitely worth it. In addition to seeing shearwaters, petrels, gulls, terns, phalaropes, skuas, and other great birds, you may also see whales.

Dress warmly for a pelagic trip and bring a waterproof outer layer — the wind and weather fifty miles offshore can be very cold and wet. A pelagic trip tends to be an all-day event, so bring ample food and drink. Bring your most powerful binoculars, but leave your spotting scope at home. Even with a shoulder mount, the deck will move too much for a scope to be useful.

That moving deck will also probably make you seasick at some point during the trip. You will have plenty of company as you hang over the leeward rail. The chances of seasickness are reduced if you stay on deck, keep your eyes on the horizon, and keep busy. This is easy to do on a pelagic trip, since the whole point is to scan the horizon looking for birds. And nothing will make you forget how lousy you feel faster than catching sight of a new bird.

Counterintuitive as it may sound, it also helps to keep your stomach full. Eat plain, easily digested foods such as apples, crackers, rolls, and the like. Avoid anything very sweet, greasy, or fried. Even if you have to force yourself, drink plenty of water or fruit juice; avoid alcohol and carbonated drinks. Also avoid looking at or getting downwind of the chum (a loathsome mixture of ripe fish heads and guts) that is sometimes dumped overboard to draw birds closer.

Nonprescription medications for motion sickness can make you drowsy, which will not do much for your birding. Some people swear by accupressure bracelets. If you know you have a real problem with seasickness, ask your doctor about prescription medications.

## NESTING COLONIES

Many pelagic birds, particularly gulls, terns, and alcids (auks), breed in crowded colonies on rocky islands and sheer cliffs near the ocean. Thousands upon thousands of birds — some colonies may have a quarter of a million members — nest right next to each other. The sheer numbers, the distinctive aroma, and the incredible cacophony add up to a memorable experience.

On the East Coast, colonies of puffins, murres, guillemots, gannets, gulls, kittiwakes and other birds are found on the rocky coasts of the maritime provinces (New Brunswick, Nova Scotia, and Prince Edward Island), Newfoundland, the Gaspé Peninsula of Quebec, and in northern Maine. On the West Coast, look for nesting colonies along the rocky Pacific Northwest coastline and Alaska. In addition to gulls, puffins, murres, guillemots, and other birds, auklets and murrelets can also be seen. As a bonus, you may also see bald eagles, ospreys, seals, whales, and other wildlife.

Many nesting colonies can be seen from land or from the many ferries that travel in these regions (particularly among the maritime provinces and along the magnificent coast of British Columbia). Unless you have or are with someone with local knowledge of the waters, it's not a good idea to visit a nesting island on your own. Many birding organizations and tour operators arrange boat trips to nesting colonies; look in the pages of the birding magazines for announcements. Be absolutely certain to wear a broad-brimmed hat if you visit a nesting colony.

## OWLING

Virtually all your birdwatching takes place during the day. Owling is the art of seeking out owls when they are most active—at night. An owling trip actually starts days before with scouting trips to locate owl roosts. Pick a likely patch of habitat (check your field guide) and explore it for signs of owls. Listen for hoots. Look for roosting places by watching for splashes of "whitewash" (owl excrement) or pellets (regurgitated undigestible matter) under tree branches. Check into rock crevices, tree cavities, and other possible roosting places. Owls tend to prefer dense vegetation, and are often found in thick conifer woods.

To catch the owl in action, trade your binoculars for a powerful flashlight with fresh batteries. Dress warmly. For optimal results, time your excursion for well after midnight, preferably the couple of hours before dawn. If you want to go owling at a more manageable hour, begin just at dusk. Spring is a particularly good time because the birds are staking out territories and nesting sites, and will be more active. Irruptive owls, of course, will be seen only in the winter. Whenever you look for owls, try to select a clear, calm, moonlit night. (If you go owling at dusk in the summer, you are also likely to see members of the nocturnal goatsucker family such as the whip-poor-will or common nighthawk.)

Walk quietly to the site you have staked out, using the flashlight to see the way. Once you reach the site, turn off the light, get comfortable, and wait. You can try playing a tape of the owl's call to draw it in but, if you are near a favorite roosting or calling site, it will turn up sooner or later on its own. Owls fly silently, so keep your eyes open for silhouettes swooping through the shadowy darkness.

To identify the owl (if you haven't already from hearing its vocalizations during your advance scouting), look for four basic clues: size, head shape, iris color, and plumage. Many owls are amazingly tame, sitting quietly while you approach to within a few feet. You should be able to see the details quite clearly.

Always look for size first. Owls range from very large (great horned owl) to very small (saw-whet owl), and there are only fourteen possibilities. Once you've established the size, range and habitat will narrow the field quite a bit. Bear in mind that irruptions of Arctic owls (most often snowy and great gray) are fairly common.

Examining an owl pellet gives you a pretty precise idea of what the bird has been eating. To study a pellet, break it into pieces and let it soak in a bowl of water for an hour or two. Then, using tweezers, gently pull the pieces apart in the water. Owl pellets generally contain the fur and bones of small mammals, although the feathers, claws, and beaks of birds are also sometimes found. The various types of bones can be readily recognized. Long bones are from the legs; curved bones are ribs; flat, jagged fragments are parts of the skull or shoulder; bills, teeth, jawbones, and vertebrae are unmistakable.

## HAWKWATCHING

Hawks are masters of the air, soaring and flying with incredible power and grace. They are also relatively easy to find, watch, and identify, which makes them particularly good for honing your birding skills.

The easiest way to see a lot of hawks is to look for them during the autumn migration. Starting in August and continuing through November, migrant raptors stream south down well-defined migration routes. Migrating raptors tend to follow either coastlines or mountain ridges. In the eastern United States, two of the very best hawkwatching lookouts are Cape May Point on New Jersey's Atlantic coast and Hawk Mountain Sanctuary on the Kittatinny Ridge in the Allegheny Mountains of Pennsylvania. On a typical windy fall day at Hawk Mountain, over 24,000 raptors of sixteen species may pass by. An extra bonus is that other migrating birds also pass by.

At any point along the migration routes, you may spot a flock of hawks soaring upward together in a tight spiral. What you are seeing is called a kettle or boil. The hawks are using an updraft of warm air — a thermal — to rise up effortlessly into the air.

Raptor identification requires you to take a step beyond basic identification by field mark. Generally speaking, you'll never see the birds closely enough to spot the diagnostic field marks. Raptors in flight must be identified by their flight. This usually means looking at the shape and characteristic position of the wings and the way

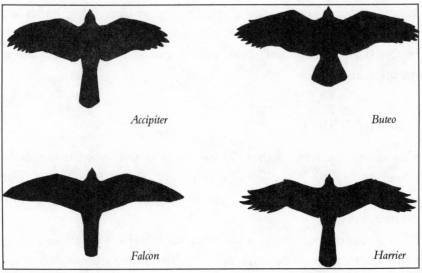

Accipiter

Buteo

Falcon

Harrier

Manuel F. Cheo

*Recognizing raptors in flight is a special skill. These silhouettes outline the basic raptor body shapes as seen from underneath. At upper left is an accipiter. Accipiters such as sharp-shinned hawks have long tails and relatively short, stubby wings. The typical buteo is shown at tupper right. Buteos, such as the very common red-tailed hawk, have shorter tails and wider wings designed for soaring. At bottom left is a falcon. These birds are designed for speed, with long, pointed wings and long tails. Harriers have slimmer wings and longer tails than buteos and are larger than accipiters.*

the birds fly — the rhythm of their wing flaps and glides — to arrive at a strong overall impression, reinforced by any behavior or field marks you might see. Because so many hawks go by during migration time, you will have ample opportunity to learn.

Prepare for an autumn visit to a hawkwatch by studying your field guide and the indispensable book *Hawks in Flight*, by Pete Dunne, David Sibley, and Clay Sutton. Pay particular attention to the silhouette drawings of birds in flight. Study the appearance of the red-tailed hawk, since this is a benchmark bird. Review the names of the wing parts and feathers — you'll be hearing a lot about wrist patches and primaries. Dress warmly. Bring your binoculars, a hat with a brim, and a cushion to sit on. The hawks go past all day long; bring food and drink. If you can, pick a day with a brisk northwest wind.

You will rarely be alone at a hawkwatching site. This is great for beginners, since there will always be someone who can identify the birds as they pass over and point out the differences and similarities to you. At many hawkwatch sites, staff members give short identification classes for beginners. Captive birds are often on hand for close-up looks.

Hawkwatchers tend to use a shorthand vocabulary. A TV is a turkey vulture; a BV is a black vulture. Sharpie is short for sharp-shinned hawk. Dihedral, a term borrowed from aviation, is sometimes used to describe the position of the wings in the gliding position when seen head-on. Technically, the dihedral is the angle formed between the wing and true horizontal or, in practical terms, the wings and the body. Kiting—holding still while facing into the wind, like a kite on the end of a string—is done only by red-tailed and ferruginous hawks. Hawk food describes any small, unidentified bird.

## DESERT BIRDING

Technically, a desert is an arid region with a limited population of specially adapted plant and animal life. By this definition, a tundra is a cold desert. In practice, desert birding refers loosely to birdwatching in hot, dry areas with low or scrubby vegetation. The chapparal areas of southern California, the hilly piñon and juniper regions of the Southwest, the sagebrush hills of Nevada and Wyoming, and the true scrub desert of the Southwest and Texas are all great places for seeing birds. And because southern California, Arizona, New Mexico, and the Rio Grande Valley of Texas border on Mexico, you have a good chance of seeing birds that usually breed in Mexico but are sometimes found in the United States. In mountainous southeastern Arizona, for example, you could see ten or more different hummingbird species, as well as elegant and eared trogons.

You can easily predict the presence of some birds in arid areas simply by their names: cactus wren, sage thrasher, scrub jay, piñon jay. Other common desert birds are roadrunner, canyon wren, elf owl, common poorwill, and vermilion flycatcher. The Southwest and the Rio Grande Valley cover a vast area. To get the most out of a birding trip, invest in one of the excellent bird-finding guides to the region.

To have a safe and productive trip, follow a few simple precautions. Dress for the weather and the terrain. Wear sturdy, ankle-high hiking boots. Lightweight clothing is essential for hot days, but remember that desert areas, particularly those at high elevations, cool off rapidly at night. Bring a sweater or jacket. Wear a hat with a brim, wear sunglasses, and use plenty of sunscreen. Bring lots of water — much more than you think you'll need — and be sure to drink it. At high elevations, the temperature may not feel that hot, but the air is very dry and you can become dehydrated without feeling overheated or thirsty.

If you're birding by yourself, be sure to have a reliable vehicle and an accurate map, particularly if you're going into a remote or rugged area. You might also want to tell someone where you're going and what your approximate schedule will be, in case of mishap.

## TROPICAL BIRDING

Only one area of the continental United States is truly tropical: southern Florida. This region, which includes Everglades National Park, Biscayne National Park, Ding Darling National Wildlife Refuge at Sanibel Island, and the Keys, is a birder's paradise. Birds of all sorts are abundant in southern Florida—a visit here is a great way to jump-start your life list. Look especially for shorebirds and waders such as brown pelicans, limpkins, reddish egrets, roseate spoonbill, wood storks, and purple gallinules. Southern Florida also has some particular specialties, such as the smooth-billed ani and gray kingbird; the white-crowned pigeon is found only in the Keys. Raptor-watchers can hope to see swallow-tailed kites; the endangered snail kite can be seen at Lake Okeechobee and the Loxahatchee National Wildlife Refuge.

At the very tip of the chain of little islands that make up the Florida Keys are several tiny islands called the Dry Tortugas. These keys are a six-hour (or more) boat ride into the Gulf of Mexico from Key West. They have no water, no accommodations, and basically no services of any sort, but they do have birds you can see nowhere else in the United States. Boobies, noddies, and tropicbirds are easily seen, and there is also a large colony of sooty terns. Because of the lack of facilities, it's best to visit the Dry Tortugas as part of a group. Trips are arranged by many birding organizations and tour operators; check the pages of the birding magazines.

Numerous excellent birdfinding guides are available for Florida. For a lyrical evocation of the Everglades region, read *River of Grass* and other works by Majorie Stoneman Douglas; for an excellent discussion illustrated by gorgeous photos, read *Everglades* by Connie Toops.

Wherever you go to bird in Florida, bring sunscreen and plenty of mosquito repellent; you'll need them.

## BACKYARD BIRDING

It's not really going afield to watch the birds in your own backyard, but it may be the easiest and most educational birding of all. Don't be put off by those who speak of backyard birders with derision. Some of the most original and important work on territoriality was done by Margaret Morse Nice, who observed the song sparrows in her Ohio backyard in the 1930s.

To observe the birds in your backyard, all you need do is look out your window. If you can put up a birdfeeder or a birdbath, so much the better. Even in large cities, you will attract a surprising variety of birds to go along with the starlings, house sparrows, and pigeons. You can practice applying the principles of bird identification to the new birds you attract, but the real joy of backyard birding is observing bird behavior. Your house or apartment is the perfect observation blind — sheltered and temperate, with bathroom and kitchen at hand. By watching the yard regularly, you will soon start to observe territorial behavior, feeding patterns, aggression, mating behavior, and much more. You may also be fortunate enough to have robins, house finches, or other birds nest where they can easily be watched. You might even learn to recognize individual birds.

Another advantage of backyard birding is that you can get very close to the birds without disturbing their normal activity. If you put up a window feeder, for example, you will be able to watch the birds from only inches away. The intimate glimpses of bird life you see in your own backyard give you a deep qualitative understanding of a relatively few bird species. As you attain a more quantitative knowledge of birds, you will quickly recognize similar behavior in unfamiliar birds.

# Checklists and Lists

Checklists, also known as field cards or trip lists, are an easy way to keep track of what you see on a birding field trip. In its most basic form, a checklist is simply a listing, in taxonomic order, of every bird found at a particular site, with a space or box next to each listing. You check off (or tick, if you are British) each bird when and if you see it on your trip. Checklists are usually more complex than just a simple listing, but this is one of the rare instances where complexity is better than simplicity.

At the main entrance to virtually any wildlife site — national and state parks, refuges, and sanctuaries — you will find a bird checklist in pamphlet form. Most are free; if there is a fee, it is nominal. A thorough checklist for a birding site is crammed with useful information. It may contain a map of the site indicating lookout points, observation towers, trails, and bathrooms. Some background information about the site is also usually included. The checklist itself lists, in taxonomic order, only those birds that have been seen at the site. Next to each bird is an indication of its seasonal appearance, its status (e.g., migrant), and its relative abundance. A list of accidental and hypothetical (unconfirmed sightings) birds may also be included.

Seasonal appearance is usually divided into the four bird-watching seasons, as follows: Spring (abbreviated as Sp or s) is March through May; summer (abbreviated Su or S) is June through

A

B

**Field Card A**

| | |
|---|---|
| Eastern B | Orange-crowned |
| Gray B | Nashville |
| Flycatcher, Scissor-tailed B | Parula, Northern B |
| Lark, Horned B | Warbler, Yellow B |
| Martin, Purple B | Chestnut-sided |
| Swallow, Tree B | Magnolia |
| N. Rough-winged B | Cape May |
| Bank B | Black-throated Blue |
| Cliff B | Yellow-rumped |
| **Cave** | **Black-throated Gray** |
| Barn B | Black-throated Green B |
| Jay, Blue B | Blackburnian |
| Crow, American B | Yellow-throated B |
| Fish B | Pine B |
| Chickadee, Carolina B | Prairie B |
| Titmouse, Tufted B | Palm |
| Nuthatch, Red-breasted | Bay-breasted |
| White-breasted B | Blackpoll |
| Brown-headed B | Cerulean B |
| Creeper, Brown | Black-and-white B |
| **Wren, Rock** | Redstart, American B |
| Carolina B | Warbler, Prothonotary B |
| *Bewick's* B | Worm-eating B |
| House B | Swainson's B |
| Winter | Ovenbird B |
| Sedge | Waterthrush, Northern |
| Marsh B | Louisiana B |
| Kinglet, Golden-crowned | Warbler, Kentucky B |
| Ruby-crowned | **Connecticut** |
| Gnatcatcher, Blue-Gray B | **Mourning** |
| **Wheatear, Northern** | Yellowthroat, Common B |
| Bluebird, Eastern B | Warbler, Hooded B |
| Veery | Wilson's |
| Thrush, Gray-cheeked | Canada |
| Swainson's | Chat, Yellow-breasted B |
| Hermit | Tanager, Summer B |
| Wood B | Scarlet B |
| Robin, American B | **Western** |
| Catbird, Gray B | Cardinal, Northern B |
| Mockingbird, Northern B | Grosbeak, Rose-breasted B |
| **Thrasher, Sage** | **Black-headed** |
| Brown B | Blue B |
| Pipit, American | Bunting, Indigo B |
| **Sprague's** | Painted B |
| Waxwing, Cedar B | Dickcissel B |
| Shrike, Loggerhead B | **Towhee, Green-tailed** |
| Starling, European B | Rufous-sided B |
| Vireo, White-eyed B | Sparrow, Bachman's B |
| **Bell's** | **American Tree** |
| Solitary B | Chipping B |
| Yellow-throated B | **Clay-colored** |
| *Warbling* B | Field B |
| Philadelphia | Vesper |
| Red-eyed B | *Lark* B |
| *Black-whiskered* | **Bunting, Lark** |
| Warbler, Blue-winged B | Sparrow, Savannah |
| Golden-winged | Grasshopper B |
| Tennessee | *Henslow's* |

**Field Card B**

| GOATSUCKERS | | | | Brown Creeper | | | |
|---|---|---|---|---|---|---|---|
| Common Nighthawk | | | | **WRENS** | | | |
| Chuck-will's-widow | | | | Carolina Wren | | | |
| Whip-poor-will | | | | Bewick's Wren | | | |
| **SWIFT & HUMMINGBIRD** | | | | House Wren | | | |
| Chimney Swift | | | | Winter Wren | | | |
| Ruby-throated Hummingbird | | | | Sedge Wren | | | |
| **KINGFISHER & WOODPECKERS** | | | | Marsh Wren | | | |
| Belted Kingfisher | | | | **KINGLETS, GNATCATCHER & THRUSHES** | | | |
| Red-headed Woodpecker | | | | Golden-crowned Kinglet | | | |
| Red-bellied Woodpecker | | | | Ruby-crowned Kinglet | | | |
| Yellow-bellied Sapsucker | | | | Blue-gray Gnatcatcher | | | |
| Downy Woodpecker | | | | Eastern Bluebird | | | |
| Hairy Woodpecker | | | | Veery | | | |
| Northern Flicker | | | | Gray-cheeked Thrush | | | |
| Pileated Woodpecker | | | | Swainson's Thrush | | | |
| **FLYCATCHERS** | | | | Hermit Thrush | | | |
| Olive-sided Flycatcher | | | | Wood Thrush | | | |
| Eastern Wood-Pewee | | | | American Robin | | | |
| Yellow-bellied Flycatcher | | | | **MOCKINGBIRDS & THRASHER** | | | |
| Acadian Flycatcher | | | | Gray Catbird | | | |
| Alder Flycatcher | | | | Northern Mockingbird | | | |
| Willow Flycatcher | | | | Brown Thrasher | | | |
| Least Flycatcher | | | | **PIPIT & WAXWING** | | | |
| Eastern Phoebe | | | | Water Pipit | | | |
| Great Crested Flycatcher | | | | Cedar Waxwing | | | |
| Eastern Kingbird | | | | **SHRIKE & STARLING** | | | |
| **LARK & SWALLOWS** | | | | Loggerhead Shrike | | | |
| Horned Lark | | | | European Starling | | | |
| Purple Martin | | | | **VIREOS** | | | |
| Tree Swallow | | | | White-eyed Vireo | | | |
| N. Rough-winged Swallow | | | | Solitary Vireo | | | |
| Bank Swallow | | | | Yellow-throated Vireo | | | |
| Cliff Swallow | | | | Warbling Vireo | | | |
| Barn Swallow | | | | Philadelphia Vireo | | | |
| **JAY & CROWS** | | | | Red-eyed Vireo | | | |
| Blue Jay | | | | **WARBLERS** | | | |
| American Crow | | | | Blue-winged Warbler | | | |
| Fish Crow | | | | Golden-winged Warbler | | | |
| Common Raven | | | | Tennessee Warbler | | | |
| **CHICKADEES & TITMOUSE** | | | | Orange-crowned Warbler | | | |
| Black-capped Chickadee | | | | Nashville Warbler | | | |
| Carolina Chickadee | | | | Northern Parula | | | |
| Tufted Titmouse | | | | Yellow Warbler | | | |
| **NUTHATCHES & CREEPER** | | | | Chestnut-sided Warbler | | | |
| Red-breasted Nuthatch | | | | Magnolia Warbler | | | |
| White-breasted Nuthatch | | | | Cape May Warbler | | | |
| Brown-headed Nuthatch | | | | Black-throated Blue Warbler | | | |

*A checklist or field card for the region in which you are birding is a valuable tool, both for recording your field trip and for identifying the birds you see. All checklists list only those birds that have been found (no matter how rarely) in the area covered. All checklists are organized taxonomically and provide a space by the species name for a tick mark. Beyond that, field cards vary widely in the information they provide. Field card A, for example, is in the minimalist tradition. It indicates species that have been in the region only very rarely in boldface or italics; species known to breed in the region are indicated with a letter B. Field card B takes much the same approach, but provides enough*

C

D

BLACK-CAPPED
CHICKADEE

| | | |
|---|---|---|
| Wren, Bewick's* | P | Mu WRu(ce,s) SRr |
| House* | P | Mfc WRu(esp. s) SRLfc(esp. nw) |
| Winter | 10A-4D + | WRfc |
| Sedge° | P | SRvr(e, nw) Mfc WRu(s) |
| Marsh | 9D-5D | Mfc WRu(s) |
| **KINGLETS TO GNATCATCHER** | | |
| Kinglet, Golden-crowned | 9D-4D + | WRfc |
| Ruby-crowned | 9D-5D | WRc(esp. s,ce) |
| Gnatcatcher, Blue-gray* | 3B-10D + | SRc WVr(s) |
| **BLUEBIRDS TO THRASHER** | | |
| Bluebird, Eastern* | P | c |
| Veery | 4C-5D + | Mu |
| Thrush, Gray-cheeked | 4B-5D + | Mfc |
| Swainson's | 4A-5D 9B-10D + | SpMc FMu |
| Hermit | 10B-5A + | WRc(esp.ce,s) |
| Wood* | 3D-10D | SRc |
| Robin, American* | P | c |
| Catbird, Gray* | 4B-12D + | SRc WRr(s) |
| Mockingbird, Northern* | P | c |
| Thrasher, Brown* | P | SRc WRc(esp. s) |
| **PIPITS TO STARLING** | | |
| Pipit, American | 9D-5D | Mfc WRfc(esp. s) |
| Sprague's | 10A-4C | WRvr |
| Waxwing, Cedar° | 9D-6B + | WRc |
| Shrike, Loggerhead* | P | WRc SRfc |
| Starling, European* | P | c |
| **VIREOS** | | |
| Vireo, White-eyed* | 3C-11D + | SRc |
| Bell's* | 4B-9D | Mfc SRfc(esp. n) |
| Solitary | 9A-6A | Mfc WRu(s) |

| | | |
|---|---|---|
| Vireo, Yellow-throated* | 3C-10B | SRfc |
| Warbling* | 3D-10D | SRLu |
| Philadelphia | 4A-5D 9B-10D + | Mfc |
| Red-eyed* | 3D-10B | SRc |
| **WOOD WARBLERS** | | |
| Warbler, Blue-winged* | 4A-10B | Mfc SRLu(n) |
| Golden-winged | 4C-5D 9A-10B | Mu |
| Tennessee | 4A-5D 9A-10D | Mc |
| Orange-crowned | 9A-5D | Mfc WRu(s) |
| Nashville | 3D-5D 8D-11B | Mc |
| Parula, Northern* | 3B-10C + | SRfc |
| Warbler, Yellow* | 4C-10A | Mc SRLu(n) |
| Chestnut-sided | 4C-6A 8D-10B | SpMfc FMu |
| Magnolia | 4D-6A 9B-10D | SpMfc FMu |
| Cape May | 4D-5D 9B-11D + | Mr(esp. e,ce) |
| Black-throated Blue | 5C-5D 9C-10C | Mvr(e,ce) |
| Yellow-rumped | 9C-5C | WRc |
| Black-thr. Green | 3D-5D 8B-11A + | SpMc FMu |
| Blackburnian | 4A-6A 9A-10B | SpMfc FMu |
| Yellow-throated* | 3B-10C + | SRfc |
| Pine* | P | c(esp. ce,s) |
| Prairie* | 4A-9C | SRc |
| Palm | 4A-5B 9A-12D + | SpMu(Lfc esp. ne,nw) FMr |
| Bay-breasted | 4C-5D 9B-11A | Mc(esp. e) |
| Blackpoll | 4B-5D + | Mfc |
| Cerulean* | 3D-9B | SRu |
| Black-and-white* | 3A-10D + | SRc |
| Redstart, American* | 3D-10B + | Mfc SRu |
| Warbler, Prothonotary* | 3C-9C | SRc |
| Worm-eating* | 3D-10A | SRfc(esp. sc,nw) |

**J F M A M J J A S O N**

- Say's Phoebe  gh
- Ash-throated Flycatcher  u
- Tropical Kingbird  gd
- Western Kingbird  gh
- Eastern Kingbird  gd
- Scissor-tailed Flycatcher  g
- Horned Lark  dg
- Purple Martin  pdfg/N
- Tree Swallow  glwtpm/N
- Violet-green Swallow  gfwtp/N
- N. Rough-winged Swallow  lgn/N
- Bank Swallow  ln/N
- Cliff Swallow  glth/N
- Barn Swallow  glth/N
- Gray Jay  f/N
- Steller's Jay  fx/N
- Blue Jay  p
- Scrub Jay  hu//(N)
- Clark's Nutcracker  fd
- Black-billed Magpie  gw
- American Crow  gdtpb/N
- Common Raven  wide/N
- Black-capped Chickadee  w/N
- Mountain Chickadee  pw
- Chestnut-backed Chickadee  fwxph/N
- Plain Titmouse  wu
- Bushtit  up/N
- Red-breasted Nuthatch  xfp//(N)
- White-breasted Nuthatch  hf
- Brown Creeper  fxpw/N
- Rock Wren  rd/N
- Canyon Wren  r
- Bewick's Wren  u/N
- House Wren  uhw/N
- Winter Wren  fxwp/N
- Marsh Wren  mgw/N
- American Dipper  l/N
- Golden-crowned Kinglet  fxp/N
- Ruby-crowned Kinglet  wptfx
- Blue-gray Gnatcatcher  wt
- Western Bluebird  hg/(N)
- Mountain Bluebird  g
- Townsend's Solitaire  wftpx
- Swainson's Thrush  wf/N
- Hermit Thrush  xftuw/(N)

space to use the card for three separate field trips (or three different sites on the same trip). A more informative field card — indeed, this one may be too informative — is shown in example C. This card uses a complex system of abbreviations to indicate the seasonal presence, preferred habitat, relative abundance, and region of the state for each species. Bar graphs are used in field card D to indicate seasonal status; the letters after the species name indicate preferred habitat. Checklists that indicate abundance and habitat are very helpful to birders. If you know that a particular species is abundant for the season and habitat, you are much more likely to see and identify it.

August; fall (abbreviated F) is September through November; and winter (abbreviated W) is December through February. Some checklists, particularly those along coastal flyways that get a lot of migrants, shorten summer to end in mid-July and divide fall into two parts: early fall (abbreviated EF) is from mid-July to mid-September; late fall (abbreviated LF) is from mid-September through November.

Status indicates the nature of a bird's presence at the site. Status categories are usually broken down as follows: Permanent resident (abbreviated P) means that individuals of the species are present in all seasons; migrant (abbreviated M) indicates species that move through the site in spring and fall; breeding (abbreviated B or indicated by an asterisk or other symbol) means that the species is known to breed at the site; transient (abbreviated T) indicates a nonbreeding species at the site as a temporary visitor (usually in the winter or summer).

Relative abundance is an indication of the number of individuals of a species likely to be seen. Abundance categories tend to be a little loose, but the following terms generally apply: Abundant, meaning that numbers of the bird are easily observed at any time; common, meaning that the bird is very likely to be seen or heard during the proper season in suitable habitat; uncommon, meaning that the bird is present during the proper season but may not be seen; occasional, meaning that the bird is seen only a few times during a season; scarce, meaning that the bird is seen only once every few seasons; rare, meaning that the bird is usually not present and is seen at intervals of two to five years; and accidental, meaning that there is only one existing record of the bird at the site.

The birds in the checklist are listed down the left-hand side of the page, with a space for the check mark to the left of each species. The seasons are listed across the top of each page to the right of the species list. Status and abundance are indicated to the right of each species, under the appropriate season. Generally the abbreviations discussed above are used, either singly or in combination, to indicate the relative abundance of a species during each season and its status. Sometimes the relative abundance is given in a more directly visual way by a horizontal bar across the seasons. The width of the bar from top to bottom indicates abundance. The thicker the bar, the more abundant the bird.

This may all sound more confusing than helpful but, to a beginning birder, a good checklist is a godsend. Glance over the checklist before beginning your field trip to get an idea of what to expect from the site. If you know from the checklist that you should be looking for breeding glossy ibis in the spring, for example, you are more likely to see them and to identify them immediately as glossy ibis. More importantly for beginners, the checklist helps you quickly eliminate your wilder guesses about a bird's identity. If you think you have spotted a Wilson's phalarope at Jamaica Bay in late fall, a glance at the checklist tells you that this bird is rare for the time and place. You can thus eliminate Wilson's phalarope from consideration and concentrate on figuring out what sort of sandpiper the bird really is (stilt, probably).

As a beginning birder, you may not be able to pin down your identifications to a species within a family. You may be able to identify a bird as a member of the wren family, for example, but not beyond that. In such cases, you should still make a checklist notation. In the margin near the family in question (or elsewhere if there isn't room), write wren sp. (short for species). If you see more than one unidentified species, use the plural abbreviation spp.

Perhaps the most important abbreviation a novice birder needs for a checklist is the frequently used LBB, which stands for little brown bird. Variations include LYB for little yellow bird and LBJ for little brown job. Another common abbreviation is BVD, for better view desired. Don't be embarassed to enter these on your checklist — if more experienced birders do it, so can you.

In addition to the information provided on the checklist, you should add some of your own. Note the number of individuals seen in a species — e.g., you saw six cardinals or a flock of Canada geese estimated at two hundred. If you can, indicate sex and age by your check marks. Note the date and time of your trip, the weather conditions, the route you took, who you went with, any interesting behavior you may have seen, and anything else that seems relevant. Count up the total number of species seen and heard. If you see a life bird on the trip, you will certainly want to note that. You can also purchase inexpensive blank checklists (both North American and regional) from the American Birding Association (see Appendix B) and fill in the categories yourself.

Your checklists contain lots of valuable information — never discard them. Checklists from previous visits to a particular site are very useful when you are planning a return trip. Use the old checklist to draw up a list of the birds you missed the last time, for example, or to decide on a different route.

## LISTS

Listing is an integral part of birdwatching, one that provides a great deal of harmless fun and also helps make you a better birder.

### Life lists

Virtually all birders keep a life list — that is, a list of all the bird species they have ever seen. A fairly serious birdwatcher can easily have a life list that tops 300 species, while a really serious birder will have seen at least 500. A number of the best birders in North America have passed the 600-species milestone, and some have surpassed 700 of the approximately 840 possible North American species. The world record for bird species seen is now held by Harvey Gilston of Switzerland, who has seen more than 7,069 of the possible 9,600 or so species. Phoebe Snetsinger of the United States broke the 7,000 mark in 1992.

As a beginner, you will probably want to concentrate on building up your life list, adding as many species as possible. This is fairly easy to do at first, when every bird is new to you, but you will slow down a bit after you get to the first hundred or so. To add new birds more quickly, you will probably have to travel outside your local area. To get much over two hundred life birds, you will certainly have to travel, at least within your state and probably farther afield.

Your life list should be more than just check marks on a preprinted list. Many birders keep detailed records about their life birds, including the date, time, place, circumstances, and sighting notes.

Follow these rules when adding birds to your life list: Count only birds that you have seen since you started the list. Add a bird to the list only if you feel you have positively identified it by yourself and would be able to identify it again. Don't count partial glimpses of birds identified by others. Only unrestrained, native, living birds should be counted — captive or dead birds of any sort are out, as are escaped exotic birds. (But what about the well-established, free-living colonies of monk parakeets found in Bridgeport, Connecticut, and Warwick, Rhode Island? Not yet.) Finally, only count the bird if it was observed under ethical conditions (see the ABA Code of Ethics in Appendix A). In all aspects of listing, let your conscience be your guide.

Should you count a heard-only bird on your life list? This is an extremely controversial question in higher birding circles, and one that has no definitive answer. The American Birding Association, arbiter of North American listing standards and records, at present says heard-only birds don't count on life lists for the ABA area and the world, but do count on all other lists — regional, local, and others. On the other hand, similar organizations in other countries accept heard-only birds, and heard-only birds are accepted in Christmas and Big Day counts. In the end, the decision is up to you — but see the sections on birding ethics and using sound to attract birds before you make up your mind.

Handicapped birders, of course, should have no hesitation about including heard-only birds — or even felt-only birds — on their life lists.

## Listing regions

Most birders actually keep two basic life lists: an American Birding Association Area list and a World List. The ABA checklist area includes Canada and the forty-nine continental United States and their adjacent waters to a distance of two hundred miles or half the distance to a non-included area, whichever is less. The southern offshore limit is the latitude of the Mexican border. The birds of the ABA Area are defined by the ABA Checklist Committee. The birds of the world are defined by the latest edition of *Birds of the World: A Checklist*, by James F. Clements. The fourth edition of this work, usually referred to in birders' shorthand as just Clements, was published in 1991.

In addition to the ABA checklist area, there are nine ABA listing regions: the six continents and their offshore waters, and the three major oceans. By this definition, North America includes all of

Canada and the continental United States below the Arctic Circle, the Caribbean region, and Mexico and the rest of Central America. (The Arctic is part of the Atlantic region; Hawaii is part of the Pacific region.)

The ABA listing areas are often broken down by listers into slightly smaller geographic subdivisions such as the lower forty-eight or fifty states, New England, and the like.

An alternative to the ABA checklist area is the checklist of North American birds published by the American Ornithologists Union (AOU). Geographically, this list covers the region from the Arctic through Panama, including the West Indies and Hawaii. The AOU checklist also assigns a number to every species. These numbers are widely used in the ornithological world for scientific work, but they can be more than a little confusing to beginners.

## Other lists

Listing can go far, far beyond the life list — Roger Tory Peterson keeps a list of all the birds he has ever seen or heard in movies. The more usual sorts of lists are generally restricted by time, place, or some combination of the two. Many birders keep a year list, tallying all the species seen in a calendar year; they also often keep state or locality lists and a property or neighborhood list. Time and place lists can be narrowed further. Time lists, for example, could include seasonal totals, monthly totals, totals on a particular day from year to year, even birds seen on your birthday. For an extra fillip, you can calculate averages — the average number of birds you have seen in a month, for example. The shorter the time period, the more often you can enjoy recalculating the average.

Place lists could include birds seen in a particular refuge, in the neighborhood, in the county, on the way to the weekend house, on vacations, and the like. Even more limited are lists that combine time and place: all the birds seen in a particular park at lunchtime, in the backyard by month, or at a particular hot-spot in the first week of May, for example.

Other interesting lists to keep include captive birds seen (as pets, in zoos and aviaries, at banding stations), breeding birds, birds in flight, birds seen on television, juvenile birds, dead birds (museum specimens don't count), appearance lists (first and last appearance in a season), birds photographed, a list of all your birding lists, and virtually any other combination or permutation you can imagine.

What's the point of all this? For the more obsessive birders, listing has an intrinsic pleasure that needs no further explanation. If your personality tends toward this direction, you will find listing in all its variations to be an extremely satisfying aspect of birding. Even if you tend more to the haphazard, listing adds spice to birding and helps keep your enthusiasm high. It's always interesting to compare lists, such as those from the same day and place but different years. As you approach a listing milestone — your two-hundredth bird, for example — an ordinary field trip can turn into a suspense-filled odyssey. (Definitely celebrate the attainment of a milestone.) Somehow even the most routine bird takes on new interest if seeing it means a check mark on a list of your own devising — seeing a house sparrow in every front yard in your neighborhood, say. A gap in your list can make you redouble your efforts to see a particular bird. If you have seen every member of the heron family found in the east except for the American bittern, for example, the unchecked box on your life list will haunt you until it is filled. And when it is filled, the mingled sense of joy and regret you feel is an emotion unique to birding.

## Listing tools

Most field guides contain a basic taxonomic checklist, but this is hardly adequate for even the most rudimentary life list, much less any other sort of list. Inexpensive basic checklists can be purchased from the American Birding Association and from nature stores; state and regional checklists can usually be obtained from state wildlife officials or local birding organizations. Beautifully produced life checklists, nicely printed and bound with lots of room for notes, are also available. Never buy one of these charming volumes. Once your interest in birds becomes known to your family and friends, you will receive one as a gift once every two years on average.

If you enjoy listing, you'll love computerized listing programs. Reviewed and advertised in the pages of all the birding magazines, listing programs have gone from being novelties to being routine. These relatively inexpensive, user-friendly programs are basically specialized data bases that let you keep track of your sightings and field notes and organize them in almost any way you want. This is a great boon to hard-core listers, since organizing and reorganizing lists is a favorite pastime, and it's a lot easier to do this on a computer than with index cards. Listing programs also generate useful reports and target lists. For example, if you are planning a trip to a particular locale, most programs can produce a report listing the birds found in the region, which of those birds you have already seen, and which you haven't. The target list of unseen species will help you set your goals and plan the trip.

# Optics for Birders

· · · · · · · · · · · · · · · · · · · · · · ·

*U*ntil quite recently, a birdwatcher's most important piece of equipment was a shotgun. John James Audubon, for example, routinely shot his specimens, stuffed them, and then used wires to arrange the corpses into lifelike positions for painting them. Ornithologists both before and after Audubon followed the same procedure, amassing study collections of bird specimens that are still of great value to modern researchers. Indeed, birds are sometimes still shot for quite valid research purposes today.

In Audubon's day and for decades thereafter, telescopes and field glasses were cumbersome, heavy, and image-distorting. Since about the turn of the century, however, great improvements in optical engineering have led to binoculars and spotting scopes that are light, easy to use, and provide sharp, accurate detail.

## BINOCULARS

A really good pair of binoculars is the single most important investment a birdwatcher can make. Really good binoculars are expensive. As a beginner, you may be reluctant to spend hundreds of dollars for superior optics when you can buy binoculars bearing the name of one of several well-known Japanese camera companies for much less. Or you may already have binoculars that were obtained for some other reason years ago. You have a good point — if your

*Courtesy Carl Zeiss Optical, Inc.*

*The evolution of modern binoculars is shown in this photo. At right is a pair of Zeiss 18 × 50 binoculars from 1914 — basically two small field glasses placed side by side. At center is the modern day Zeiss 8 × 56 model. At left is the latest in binocular technology: 20 × 60 binoculars with an internal stabilization system. These powerful binoculars can be hand held.*

commitment to birdwatching is only of the most casual sort. If it is anything more than that, spend the money.

The point of outstanding binoculars is not that you will see more birds—although you may—but that you will see them more accurately. Inexpensive optics distort the image and the colors. Just as a mediocre pianist sounds much better and enjoys it more when playing a fine grand piano than a battered upright, beginning birders find and identify more birds with good binoculars than poor ones.

It's also more cost-effective to buy good binoculars at the start, because you will buy them in the end anyway. Skip the inevitable period of increasing dissatisfaction and frustration that comes with

*The 8 × 42 Natureview binoculars from Bushnell have been endorsed by the National Audubon Society. These binoculars offer excellent optics at a very reasonable cost.*

*Courtesy Bausch & Lomb*

crummy binoculars and go right for the good ones. Carefully chosen, high-quality binoculars can last a lifetime. As with any expensive purchase, be informed and shop around before you buy your new binocs. To help, below are short explanations of the important basic concepts and technical terms.

*Outstanding optics are expensive but worth every penny. This model is the 10 × 42 Elite from Bausch & Lomb.*

*Courtesy Bausch & Lomb*

## Magnification

Binoculars are often described by their magnification and lens diameter; for example, 7 x 50. The first number in this equation indicates the magnification. Thus binoculars that magnify seven times (7x) will make objects appear to be seven times closer — that is, a bird that is 70 feet away will appear to be only 10 feet away when seen through the binoculars. Binoculars ranging from 7x to 10x are ideal for birding.

## Lens diameter

The second number in the description 7 × 50 indicates the diameter of the lens (also called the objective) in millimeters (multiply by 0.04 for the equivalent in inches). Since bigger objectives gather more light, the larger the lens the brighter the image and the better you can see in dim light. Bigger objectives also mean more resolution — you can see finer details. On the other hand, the bigger the

*These 10 × 40 binoculars from Zeiss are relatively compact and light for their power.*

*Courtesy Carl Zeiss Optical, Inc.*

objectives the heavier the binoculars. Birders tend to choose binoculars that are 7 × 35, 7 × 50, 8 × 40, or 10 × 42 because these sizes offer good compromises between magnification, brightness, and weight.

## Field of view

The size, expressed in degrees (angular field) or feet or meters (linear field), of the area you can see through a pair of binoculars is called the field of view. In either case, the larger the field of view the larger the area that appears in the image. A wide field of view is useful when observing things, like birds or sports, that are likely to move; the narrower the field of view, the more often you will have to move and refocus the binoculars to keep the subject in view. Field of view is relative to magnification. The greater the magnification, the smaller the field of view usually is. Field of view is usually indicated on the body of the binoculars in degrees, feet, and meters. For example, the marking "8° 410 ft at 1000 yds" indicates that the field of view encompasses eight degrees of an imaginary circle with you at the center; at 1,000 yards the field of view is 410 feet wide. Birders prefer binoculars with as wide a field of view as possible without distortion at the edges. At the minimum, purchase binoculars with a field of view of at least 250 feet at 1,000 yards.

## Exit pupil

If you hold the binoculars at arm's length up to a light, you will see a small circle containing an image in the eyepiece. This circle is known as the exit pupil. In general, the bigger the exit pupil the brighter the image. Optimally, its diameter should match the maximum size the pupil of your eye can dilate (widen) to under the lighting conditions you are most likely to encounter. If the exit pupil is the same size as your pupil, all the light transmitted by the binoculars enters your eye and you get a bright image. If the exit pupil is larger than your pupil, some of the light falls on the iris and is wasted. If the exit pupil is smaller than your pupil, you may have difficulty keeping the image centered in your eye.

Under very dim conditions the eye's pupil can open to a diameter no wider than about one-quarter of an inch (7 mm). Thus binoculars that would be useful for observations in early dawn or twilight conditions would have an exit pupil that size; with an exit pupil of only an eighth or 3/16th of an inch (4 to 5 mm), the binoculars would be useful only in full daylight. However, the eye's ability to dilate decreases with age. For middle-aged and older people, some of the light coming through the eyepiece may fall outside the pupil of the eye and not be perceived.

Because your pupils contract in bright light, binoculars with bigger objectives that gather more light will be no brighter when birdwatching on a sunny beach, for example, than binoculars with smaller objectives and the same magnification. If, on the other hand, you do a lot of your birding in shady woods or in twilight, a bigger exit pupil will be a definite asset. Bigger exit pupils are also helpful when you are birding from a moving platform — a boat, for example — since the larger exit pupil is easier to keep centered over your own pupil. As a rule, you will have more flexibility if you select binoculars with a bigger exit pupil.

Important as it is, the exit pupil number is not marked on binoculars. Ask the salesperson, or check the descriptive specifications provided by the manufacturer.

The appearance of the exit pupil also lets you assess the quality of the prisms. All binoculars use prisms to orient the image correctly; otherwise, you would see things upside-down through the binoculars. Look carefully at the shape of the exit pupil. In the best binoculars, the exit pupils are perfect circles centered in the eyepiece, indicating high-quality prisms accurately aligned. In lesser binoculars, the prisms can produce exit pupils that are elongated, off-center, or have the edges cut off, making them look like square pegs in round holes. The result is dim, distorted, or vignetted images. (See below for more about prisms.)

### Relative brightness index (RBI)

Brightness is the amount of light that exits the binoculars and enters your eyes. A certain amount of light loss is inevitable as the light passes through the complex arrangement of glass in the binoculars. The better the binoculars, the less the light loss; good modern binoculars transmit ninety percent or more of the light. The less the light loss, the brighter, and thus more accurate and detailed, the image. To determine the relative brightness index, simply square the exit pupil size in millimeters. RBI is not really a very useful number for comparing brightness between binoculars, but it is one often used by manufacturers. Another number sometimes used by manufacturers is relative light efficiency—basically the RBI raised arbitrarily by fifty percent. This is supposedly a measure of the increased light-transmitting efficiency of coated lenses as compared to uncoated lenses. All modern binoculars have coated lenses, however, and this figure is essentially meaningless if not downright deceptive.

### Twilight factor

The twilight factor is a more useful relative measure of brightness, especially for birders, who are often observing under less than full daylight conditions. This number measures both viewing efficiency and image detail in twilight conditions. To calculate the factor (it is often not in the manufacturer's literature), multiply the magnification by the diameter of the objective in millimeters, and then find the square root of the product. The larger the factor, the more efficient the binoculars are in dim light. For example, 8 × 32 binoculars would have a twilight factor of 16, while 20 × 80 binoculars would have a twilight factor of 40. The 20 × 80 binoculars would thus be better for dim light conditions, even though both might have exit pupils of the same size. For dim light, a twilight factor of at least 20 is recommended.

## Near focus

The closest distance at which the binoculars can focus is called the near focus. Generally, the more powerful the binoculars the farther the near focus distance. For a good pair of 7 × 50 binoculars the near focus would be about eighteen to twenty feet. However, in the past few years excellent binoculars that focus as closely as ten feet have become available. These have been a great boon to birders, since you can find yourself within ten feet of a bird surprisingly often. In addition, these binoculars are great for butterfly watching —an area interesting to more and more birders.

## Eye relief

The distance between the outer surface of the eyepiece lens and the surface of your eye is called the eye relief. Since the surface of your eye can't actually touch the surface of the lens, eye relief can make a difference in how much of the field of view you can see. To grasp this concept, imagine peeking through a keyhole. The closer your eye is to the opening, the more of the room inside you can see. In binoculars, the longer the eye relief, the farther away your eye can be from the eyepiece and still get a full view of the field.

Long eye relief is generally useful so that you don't have to hold the binoculars so close to your eyes that your eyelashes get in the way. It is particularly important if you wear eyeglasses all the time. The lenses in your eyeglasses keep you from bringing the eyepieces close to the surface of your eye; long eye relief lets you see most of the field of view anyway.

When you can find the eye relief listed in the manufacturer's literature, it is given in millimeters. Long eye relief ranges from 15 to 17 mm; medium eye relief is between 8 and 15 mm. The abbreviation LER (for long eye relief) or (less often) the designation B type is sometimes given instead of a measurement.

The eyepieces of binoculars have soft rubber eye cups on them. If you don't wear glasses, the eye cups are useful for blocking distracting extraneous light from entering your eyes while you look through the binoculars. If you wear glasses, eye cups simply make the eye relief longer than is desirable. In either case, if necessary roll the cups down either partway or all the way to get the eye relief that suits you best.

## Prisms

Prisms are essential to binoculars, which may explain why the terminology is never really explained in the manufacturers' literature. In optics, prisms are used to change the direction of the light path through the use of internal reflection (as near total as possible). There are two types of prisms commonly used in binoculars: porro prisms (named for their inventor) and roof prisms (so called because they resemble pitched roofs). Porro prisms are used in Z-

*These 7 × 42 Ultra Lite series binoculars from Swift use porro prisms on a B-type body. They are rubber armored and focus in to about 16 feet.*

*Courtesy Swift Instruments*

body and B-body binoculars. Roof prisms are used in H-body binoculars. (See below for an explanation of body types.) As with everything else in optics, the quality of glass used in the prism affects the quality of the image. Good porro prisms are made using a high-density glass containing barium. Abbreviated BAK-4, this type of glass has a high refractive index and provides even field illumination and excellent contrast. Lesser-grade porro prisms are made with borosilicate glass, abbreviated BK-7. Binoculars made with BK-7 prisms can have gray areas that cut across the exit pupil, resulting in vignetting. But because the roof prisms in H-style binoculars have a different internal arrangement that send the light

*The B-type binoculars body is named for its leading American manufacturer, Bausch & Lomb. This example is the 8 × 36 Custom model.*

*Courtesy Bausch & Lomb*

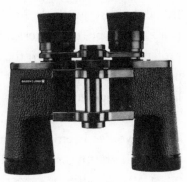

on a different path than porro prisms, they generally can't cause vignetting even when BK-7 glass is used. H-body binoculars accordingly are made using the cheaper glass with no loss of quality.

## Coatings

As light passes through the various optical elements that make up a pair of binoculars, it can be reflected around, leading to fuzzy, hazy, and low-contrast images. In addition, each element transmits slightly less than all the light that hits it, leading to dim images. Optical coatings—generally extremely thin layers of magnesium fluoride, sometimes in combination with other substances such as zirconium oxide—improve light transmission and reduce internal reflections.

Good binoculars are coated on all sides of all optical elements, with multi-coating on the objectives and eyepieces. Lousy binoculars are coated only on the outer objective and the outer eyepiece, since these are the only parts you can see without taking the binoculars apart.

## Body styles

Binoculars are available in three basic body types: the German Z (for Zeiss) type, the American B (for Bausch & Lomb) type, and the roof-prism H type (from the shape). Types Z and B binoculars use porro prisms offset from each other at a 90° angle. This sends the light entering the binoculars on a long zigzag path before it exits. The longer light path allows for larger objectives, allowing—as you know if you've been paying attention so far—higher magnifications and brighter images. Z- and B-type binoculars have the familiar offset barrels, with the objectives wider apart than the eyepieces.

*The famous Zeiss Z-type body is shown here in these compact 8 × 30 binoculars.*

*Courtesy Carl Zeiss Optical, Inc.*

Type H binoculars use roof prisms placed one behind the other, so the barrels are straight. Type H binoculars are generally light and compact, but the objectives are smaller and they are usually not as bright in dim light.

In Z-type binoculars, the objectives are in separate barrels that are screwed into the main body holding the prisms. The Z-type design is somewhat more likely to get knocked out of alignment if it is dropped. This design is also the one most often found in cheap, knock-off, no-name binoculars.

B-type binoculars have a one-piece body that is slightly sturdier. This design is also somewhat more moisture-proof. One-piece H-

*The B-type body is used on these 8× 30 perro-prism binoculars from Nikon.*

*Courtesy Nikon*

type binoculars with one-piece bodies are about as sturdy and moisture-proof as B types. However, two-piece H-type models, while sturdy, are definitely not as moisture-proof.

### Nitrogen purging

To prevent internal fogging and oxidation, the normal air inside good modern binoculars is removed and replaced with nitrogen. The process is called purging.

### Rubber armoring

Birders should invest only in binoculars with rubber or polyure-thane armoring. The advantages are many. Armored binoculars are quieter (they don't make noise and spook the birds when accidently banged against a canteen, for example) and are less likely to get dented. They are more water-resistant. They are also easier to grip when wet or cold.

### Binocular sizes

Standard binoculars weigh anywhere from about eighteen ounces to over thirty-two ounces. Compact binoculars usually weigh in at around seven to twelve ounces. Compacts are particularly handy for occasions when weight matters and birding is not the top priority — hikes, bike rides, and theatrical events. They also fit very con-veniently into the glove box of a car. Fixed-focus binoculars are not recommended for birdwatching. Avoid zoom binoculars — they are heavy, clumsy, dim, and have overall inferior optics. You will defi-nitely not see more birds with them.

*Compact binoculars are handy and surprisingly effective. This compact model is the Bausch & Lomb 7 × 26 Custom.*

*Courtesy Bausch & Lomb*

*Swift manufactures these 7 × 35 compact Audubon binoculars using roof prisms on a H-type body.*

*Courtesy Swift Instruments*

## Neck straps and other accessories

The purchase price of binoculars includes the neck strap, carrying case, and lens caps. (Beware of retailers who "strip" these from the package and sell them separately.) Immediately discard the neck strap. It is almost certainly a piece of thin plastic that will cut a permanent groove into your neck or shoulder within fifteen minutes. Replace the original strap with a broad cloth strap or, even better, a broad strap made of neoprene rubber. Make sure the strap has plastic connectors to cut down on noisy jingling and clanking. Check the strap often and replace it immediately if it starts to show signs of wear, especially where it connects to the binoculars.

Various straps and supports meant to keep binoculars from weighing down your neck and bouncing on your chest are available. They work reasonably well. A significant drawback is that you must disentangle yourself from them every time you want to take off or put on a layer of clothing.

Tripod adapters allow the binoculars to be mounted on a standard tripod for more stable, vibration-free viewing. The adapter usually screws into the front of the body hinge. The adapter socket may be covered by a little screw-in plate; don't worry if you lose it.

## USING BINOCULARS

Using your binoculars is very simple, although it does take a bit of practice to get the most out of them. Learn to use the features below.

### Interpupillary distance

This is an elaborate way of saying the space between your eyes, or more specifically, the space between the pupils. This varies from person to person, which is why binoculars have a central hinge connecting the two halves. Look through the binoculars and move the two halves together or apart until you see one clear circle of image.

### Focusing

Focus the binoculars by looking through them and using your index finger to rotate the central focusing ring found on the body hinge. Rotate to the right to focus farther in; rotate to the left to focus farther out. Porro-prism binoculars focus by moving the eyepieces in and out; roof-prism binoculars focus internally. When selecting new binoculars, make sure you can reach the focusing ring easily without shifting your grip on the binoculars.

## Diopter focus

Most people, even those with very good eyesight, see slightly better through their right eye. To accommodate the difference, a diopter (standard unit of optical measurement) adjustment mechanism is built into the right eyepiece. To adjust it, first use both eyes to focus the binoculars on something with sharp edges not too far away —a sign, for example. Close your left eye and look only through the right eyepiece. If the image is slightly out of focus, rotate the diopter adjustment until the image is sharp. Note the degree of correction by looking at the diopter or plus and minus markings on the right eyepiece. Once you have set the diopter adjustment, it stays set—you don't have to change it when you change the central focus.

## Fatigue

A few hours of keeping your arms raised while holding up your binoculars will lead to fatigue, trembling arms, and sometimes muscle cramps in the hands. Tired arms will also exaggerate the normal amount of shake transmitted to the binoculars from your body. Lighter binoculars sometimes help, but the fatigue really comes from the weight of your arms, not your binoculars. You can try propping your elbows on something—a handy fencepost—but this will exaggerate body shake. For extended viewing of a specific spot such as a nest, a tripod is a good idea.

Eye fatigue is a big problem for birders and can lead to nasty headaches. The best way to reduce eye fatigue is to use good binoculars to begin with. Remember to use the diopter adjustment. Wear polarized sunglasses on bright days. *Caution*! Never look at the sun through binoculars! Serious eye damage can result!

## Eyeglasses

If you wear eyeglasses only sometimes — just for reading or driving — or if you wear bifocals, should you keep them on or off while using binoculars? It's probably best to keep them on. You don't want to be caught fumbling around with your glasses when a good bird flies by. You also don't want to drop or lose them. If you wear prescription eyeglasses, make sure the prescription is accurate.

## Caring for binoculars

Binoculars, especially if they are armored, are surprisingly sturdy. This does not mean, however, that they can be dropped, soaked, or otherwise abused with impunity. The best way to avoid disaster is always to keep the strap around your neck or over your shoulder. Some high-quality binoculars now come with built-in, flip-up lens caps for the eyepieces. This is very helpful for keeping the eyepieces dry on wet days. Traditional individual eyepiece covers are more trouble than they are worth in the field. Put them on, along with the objective covers, when you store the binoculars. The carrying case is handy if you are packing the binoculars in a suitcase for a long trip; otherwise, forget about it. Birders always want their binoculars to be where they can get at them immediately. Water and mud should be gently wiped away with a soft cloth. Use lens cleaning fluid on the objectives and eyepieces. Never place the fluid directly on the lens. Instead, place a drop or two on a piece of lens tissue and rub the lens gently in a circular motion from the center out. A good alternative to lens fluid is a microwoven cleaning cloth, easily available at any camera store.

After birding in very cold weather, avoid bringing your binoculars indoors immediately. This can cause damaging condensation. Leave them in a cooler part of the house such as the mud room for ten or twenty minutes first.

Binoculars do occasionally get damaged by being dropped or soaked. Lenses and internal optical elements can be cracked, broken, knocked out of alignment, or damaged by water (especially salt water). Even the best binoculars are not totally immune to the inroads of moisture and dust. If repair or cleaning is needed, contact the manufacturer for more information and authorized service centers. If the binoculars have been dunked, do this immediately to minimize further damage to the coatings.

## BUYING BINOCULARS

Most camera and department stores carry binoculars. Prices are usually somewhat below list and are sometimes negotiable; the sales staff is unlikely to be very knowledgeable. These stores will sometimes have good prices on low-end binoculars by well-known manufacturers. They will also sometimes offer very attractive prices on no-name or store-brand models. Avoid these "deals" at all cost. Also avoid merchandise that is obtained on the so-called "gray" market. These items — which are often well-known brands — were manufactured for sale outside the United States and Canada. They are purchased overseas through somewhat shady channels outside the authorized distributors. This means, in effect, that you have no warranty. Don't be taken in by an unusually low price.

The best way to get wide selection, knowledgeable service, and excellent prices on binoculars and other optics is to buy them from one of the excellent specialized mail-order companies that cater to birders. Check the ads in the birding magazines and write away for catalogs. The drawback to mail-order is that you don't get to handle the binoculars and decide which feels most comfortable. To get around this, look at as many models as you can by trying friends' binoculars and visiting nearby camera stores. Read the reviews of binoculars that appear in the birding magazines. If you are interested in a specific brand or model, request sales literature and spec sheets from the manufacturer.

Once you've purchased your binoculars, send in the warranty card, make a note of the serial number, and save the receipt and any other documentation. Mark the binoculars with your name in an indelible manner.

## SPOTTING SCOPES

After a few frustrating birding trips using binoculars to try to distinguish among the assorted shorebirds huddled on a distant mud flat, you will want to own a spotting scope or become very good friends with someone who does.

Essentially a compact, portable, and powerful telescope, a spotting scope is an invaluable tool for birding. Beyond about a hundred feet, binoculars can't provide distinguishing details. With a spotting scope, you pick out fine details, observe distant behavior and nests up to 200 yards away, and even see the moons of Jupiter. By adding a camera adapter, spotting scopes become powerful telephoto lenses for photography. A spotting scope is considerably more expensive than an excellent pair of binoculars, but the new dimensions it will bring to your birding make it worth every penny and then some.

Much of the terminology used to describe spotting scopes, such as exit pupil and twilight factor, is the same as that for binoculars, but there are some differences. Below are some points to bear in mind when selecting a scope.

## Types of spotting scopes

Most birders use prismatic (also called refractor) spotting scopes. These scopes basically resemble a typical small telescope. The objective lenses are in a long, offset barrel; the body contains the focusing knob, the erecting prism (otherwise the image would be upside-down), and the eyepiece. Imagine one side of a pair of very large Z-type binoculars and you are visualizing the shape of a prismatic scope. The prismatic spotting scope has separate, interchangeable eyepieces.

Prismatic zoom spotting scopes have built-in zoom eyepieces. They usually zoom from a magnification of 15x to 45x or even 60x.

*Spotting scopes are an expensive but very useful investment. This 20 × 60 model from Nikon uses a straight-through design. The knob projecting over the barrel is used for focusing.*

*Courtesy Nikon*

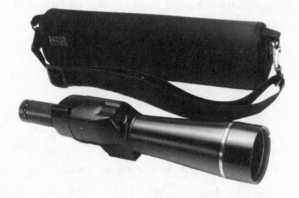

*Spotting scopes generally have objectives ranging from 50 to 90 mm. The Elite scope from Bausch & Lomb is nicely in the middle at 77 mm.*

Courtesy Bausch & Lomb

Zooms offer flexibility without having to change eyepieces. As will be discussed below, however, you may want to select different eyepieces for different circumstances. Zooms tend to be somewhat longer and heavier than regular prismatic scopes. A few manufacturers make excellent, reliable zoom scopes, but many other outstanding manufacturers do not offer the option.

Catadioptric scopes are primarily designed for astronomical viewing, but they are also widely used by nature photographers. These stubby spotting scopes use a combination of lenses and mirrors (instead of prisms) to fold the light path back and forth internally. Catadioptric scopes thus are lightweight and provide high magnification and a large aperture (f stop). In addition, a camera can be attached directly and easily to the scope; many prismatic scopes require special adapters. All these features make catadioptric scopes excellent for nature photography. When used chiefly for observing, however, the field of view is narrow, and it is hard to track a moving target. Catadioptric scopes are somewhat delicate and can be temperamental to use. For that reason, the discussion below will ignore catadioptric scopes and concentrate on regular prismatics. If observation is your primary interest, stick to a prismatic scope.

## Aperture

The diameter of the objective lens, expressed in millimeters, is the aperture of a spotting scope. As with binoculars, the bigger the aperture the brighter and more detailed the image. Generally speaking, spotting scopes for nature study have apertures ranging from 50 to 90 mm; 60 mm is a popular size.

## Magnification

Two factors determine the magnification of a spotting scope: the objective lens and the eyepiece. Magnification is determined by dividing the focal length of the objective lens by the focal length of the eyepiece. (The focal length is the distance between the lens and the point where the light passing through it converges — the focal point.) A good rule of thumb is that the useful (not theoretical) magnification of a spotting scope is about two-thirds of the aperture. For example, a 60 mm scope would have a magnification of about 40x. For most birding situations, 40x is more than adequate. As with binoculars, higher magnification means a narrower field of view and a dimmer image.

## Exit pupil

Conceptually, the exit pupil on a spotting scope is the same as it is with binoculars. The exit pupil on a scope is usually smaller. The higher the magnification, the smaller the exit pupil. To determine the size of the exit pupil with a particular eyepiece, divide the aperture by the magnification. A 60 mm aperture with a 30x eyepiece, for example, would have an exit pupil of 2 mm.

## Eyepieces

The eyepiece of a spotting scope magnifies the primary image produced by the objective lenses. Needless to say, eyepieces are critical to good performance. They are usually sold separately, although one eyepiece may be part of the deal. Because different eyepieces are appropriate for different viewing conditions, you may want to purchase at least two. With a few exceptions, eyepieces from one manufacturer will not fit into scopes from another manufacturer.

Eyepieces come in various configurations: fixed, wide-angle, and zoom (also called variable). Fixed eyepieces come in magnifications ranging from 15x to 60x, with assorted intervals in between. Wide-angle eyepieces offer fewer magnification options; they are usually available in 20x or 30x. Zoom eyepieces usually come in 15 –45x or 20–60x magnifications. Zooms are flexible, but the field of view is generally narrower. In addition, the image is often less bright because it must pass through additional optical elements. As you zoom in, depth of field (the portion of the image that is in focus from front to back) diminishes, as does the exit pupil.

Eye relief is important when choosing eyepieces. The principles are exactly the same as for binoculars. The higher the magnification on the eyepiece, the less the eye relief—a problem for eyeglass wearers who want to work at high magnifications. The abbreviation LER in the manufacturer's literature means long eye relief.

The mounting system for the eyepiece varies from manufacturer to manufacturer. Some use a bayonet mount, others use screw-in mounts or set screws. Avoid set screws, since these can be a problem in the field. The choice of bayonet or screw mount is an individual one, although some birders feel that the bayonet mount is a little easier to use.

### Eyepiece placement

The eyepiece on a spotting scope can be placed in a straight line with the objective or offset at a 45° angle. The placement makes no difference to the optics, but it can affect your viewing comfort. Straight-through designs are easier to aim (just sight down the barrel), easier to use when mounted on a car window, and easier to use for photography. On the other hand, if you are tall you will have to raise your tripod quite high to see through the scope without getting onto your knees. A tripod extended to its full length can be unstable, especially on uneven surfaces.

Offset eyepieces let you bend over to view the image. For extended viewing, this may be more comfortable. Offset eyepieces also make it easier for several people of different heights to share the scope, since the tripod height doesn't have to be constantly adjusted.

### Twilight Factor

The twilight factor in spotting scopes has the same importance as it does in binoculars.

### Focusing

Three types of focusing systems are found on spotting scopes. Helical focusers are collars on the barrel or eyepiece of the scope. Rotating the collar changes the focus quickly. Rocker-arm focusers are usually located on the top of the scope. The focus is changed very quickly by rocking the arm back and forth. Knob focusers are located on the top or rear of the scope. Rotating the knob changes the focus. Because knob focusers require more turns to change the focus significantly, they are both slower and more accurate than helical collars or rocker arms. Personal preference should guide your choice. If you will be switching back and forth between binoculars and scope a lot, you may prefer to use knob focus to avoid confusion.

### Near focus

Spotting scopes are meant for observing at a distance. The nearest focus for a typical scope is generally about twenty to twenty-five feet. For anything closer, use your binoculars.

### F stop

Because spotting scopes are so often used as telephoto lenses, the f stop is generally indicated in the sales literature.

### Other factors

Most spotting scopes come with built-in sunshades for the objective lens. Cases are usually a separate item. All scopes have quarter-inch, twenty-thread adapter screws for attaching them to tripods. Telephoto attachments for 35 mm cameras are available for most models.

## USING SPOTTING SCOPES

Spotting scopes are most valuable where the landscape is fairly open and the birds are visible and relatively still—coastlines, tidal marshes, wetlands, and the like — or for observing fixed points such as nests. They are not very helpful in wooded areas or for tracking fast-moving birds.

Don't try to search for birds with the scope as if it were binoculars. Instead, use your binoculars to sweep the area and note the location of birds you want to study further. Set up the scope and tripod on as flat an area as you can, adjusting the legs as necessary to compensate for unevenness. Make sure the tripod is stable before doing anything else. In windy conditions, try to keep one hand on the tripod at all times.

Aiming the spotting scope can be difficult at first, especially if you use one with an offset eyepiece. To aim a straight-through scope, simply look down the outside of the barrel. To aim an offset scope, use the built-in device provided by the manufacturer. This could be a line-of-sight peep bar, a peep sight, or a notch-and-bead sight (also called an iron sight) that runs parallel to the sighting axis of the scope. Look along or through the device and move the tripod head until the sight is directly on your target. When you look through the eyepiece, you should find the bird right in the center. With a little practice, you will be able to get the bird in your sights quickly every time.

On a typical birding trip, you will move the scope and tripod to a number of different sites. You don't need to take the scope off the tripod every time you move on. Before picking the combination up, however, make sure the scope is snugly attached to the tripod head. If you are on foot, carrying the scope/tripod combination can be awkward (especially on narrow trails) and tiring. Try to avoid snagging vegetation and banging into trees and other people. Watch your footing. If you are driving from point to point, you will be moving the scope/tripod into and out of the car a lot. Try laying the combination across the back seat.

To help you set up your tripod quickly, extend the legs to the correct height and then mark the spot with paint, typewriter correction fluid, or some other easily visible and waterproof substance.

## BUYING SPOTTING SCOPES

Only large, well-stocked camera stores will carry spotting scopes, so you will probably have to purchase yours through the mail. This is a very big purchase, so get as much information as you can and shop around. Prices for the same model can vary a lot. Compared to binoculars, there are fewer manufacturers and options to choose from, so it's a little easier to make up your mind.

## TRIPODS

For any viewing through a spotting scope a tripod is a necessity. Spotting scopes magnify *everything*—including body vibrations and wind shake, and they are far too heavy to hold in your hand for long. If you've just spent a small fortune to buy the spotting scope of your dreams, get a good sturdy tripod to support it. Select a tripod that is solid, with as little wobble as possible. The heavier the tripod, the more it will damp out vibrations. You don't have to buy a monster heavy-duty model, but do select one that weighs at least three pounds. Three different systems are used for adjusting leg height on a tripod. Twist collars are rotated to release and tighten the legs; flip-lock levers (also called clamp levers) flip open and close; twist locks (also called lever locks) screw in, rather like set screws. As usual, the different systems have advantages and drawbacks. Twist collars are slower but have no protruding parts to catch on things. Flip-lock levers and twist locks are faster but have protruding parts. Twist locks can get gummed up with grit.

The center post height on a tripod can be adjusted by means of a geared crank or by a locking knob. Again, personal preference dictates the choice.

The spotting scope connects to the tripod at the head, which is detachable. Virtually all heads today are fluid-damped — that is, they are filled with a thick, silicon-based grease to provide smooth, even panning when tracking birds. Select a tripod that has just one arm for controlling horizontal and vertical movement, so viewing doesn't have to be interrupted by fumbling to make adjustments. Knobs on the tripod let you lock the panning and vertical motions. A quick-release system on the head is handy because it allows the scope to be attached and removed quickly and easily, even while wearing gloves.

When selecting a tripod, check its minimum and maximum heights. The minimum height is usually anywhere between 24 and 34 inches, while the maximum ranges from 60 to 75 inches. If you are tall and use a straight-through spotting scope, you need a tripod that extends farther. However, the taller and more extended a tripod is, the more unstable it is as well.

Tripods are generally made of anodized aluminum to save weight and avoid corrosion problems. Many models are available in either chrome or black. Choose black, since it doesn't reflect sunlight that might spook the birds.

## Tripod Accessories

You may want to invest in a tripod bag or case, especially if you plan to check the tripod through as baggage when you travel by plane. Sturdy tripod straps for carrying the assembled scope and tripod make hauling them around a lot easier.

## OTHER SUPPORTS

Table-top tripods, also called shooter's stands, are compact, sturdy, and rigid. They rarely rise much more than 16 inches. They are handy if you need to set up the scope on the hood or roof of your car, but you can easily live without one.

Monopods are basically adjustable poles with a pan head attached. They are much lighter than tripods, but obviously are not as stable and can't be used for hands-free viewing. Use a monopod only with low-powered optics — there's too much vibration for anything high-powered.

There are times when a tripod is just inconvenient — too heavy to carry on a long hike, too awkward on a boat, or too slow to adjust for fast-moving birds. Shoulder mounts are a good option in these circumstances. The spotting scope is mounted onto a lightweight adjustable frame with a handgrip at the front and a rifle-style shoulder stock at the rear. As with monopods, use shoulder mounts only with low-powered optics.

Window mounts are tripod heads attached to a clamp that fits over the top edge of your car window (you have to roll the window down at least halfway). Window mounts are great for times when the weather is really bad, since you can sit comfortably in your car and still birdwatch.

# Birding in the Field

· · · · · · · · · · · · · · · · · · · · · · ·

*Y*ou've grasped the basic concepts of field identification; you know where the birds are; your binocular lenses are sparkling. It's time to go birding.

## FIELD TRIPS

As a beginner, you will spend a lot of time focusing excitedly on clumps of dead leaves, stubs of broken branches, rags and pieces of plastic clinging to fences, old newspapers stuck in bushes, and quivering twigs a bird has just flown from. Many of the warblers you see will turn into house sparrows on closer inspection; the peregrine falcons will turn out to be herring gulls. This can be frustrating beyond description, particularly when you *know* that there are lots of good birds in the area because they are singing tauntingly all around you. Keep looking. To a degree, artistry in birding is achieved only like artistry in anything else: practice, practice, practice.

And just as beginning (and even professional) musicians take lessons, birdwatchers learn from more experienced birders. By far the best way to get a good lesson in birding is to go on a bird walk or field trip with an experienced leader. You can do this easily in your own locale with your local bird club. You can also attend field trips and workshops sponsored by birding organizations. The annual spring and fall weekends sponsored by New Jersey

Audubon at Cape May, for example, draw hundreds of friendly and enthusiastic birders from all over the country and even overseas. New birders are as welcome as old hands.

A good field trip leader combines encyclopedic knowledge with good humor, patience, and a lucky streak. The leader's goal is to make sure that everyone on the trip sees as many birds as possible. Don't let diffidence hold you back. If everyone else has spotted the bird and you still haven't, say so — quietly and without a lot of arm-waving. The leader and the rest of the group will make an extra effort to help you see it.

Often, when someone spots a bird, he or she will say helpfully, "It's in the top left quadrant of that tree," while gesturing vaguely ahead. Amazingly to the novice, everyone else in the group immediately trains their binoculars exactly on the bird. In fact, this happens because several people have sighted the bird simultaneously, or because they already suspected there was something in that tree. If you still can't see the bird, look in the same general direction as everyone else while listening for further bulletins from the group. These take the shape of a continuing stream of behavior reports ("It's pecking at the branch" or "It's scratching its head"), movement reports ("It just hopped down a little" or the dreaded "It just flew"), identification reports ("Looks like a gray-cheeked thrush" countered by "Can't be. No eye ring. Must be Swainson's"), and admiration ("Just look at the color on that indigo bunting!"). You will also hear at least one other member of the group announce that he or she can't see it. At this point, additional aiming bulletins begin. Birders often use the clock system to pinpoint a location, so the bulletin might be "It's at two o'clock in the hickory tree." Alternatively and less helpfully, the reference point might be a peculiarity of the spot, along the lines of "It's just to the left of that big splintered branch." Again, if you haven't spotted the bird yet, say so. Additional directions that lead you through a series of obvious reference points until you reach the bird come next: "See the gate? See the stump just to the left of it? Now look in the lower right branches of the small tree by the big rock about twenty feet to the left of the stump. Got it?" As a desperate last measure, finger-pointing or even a yank into a better viewpoint will be forthcoming. Eventually the bird will fly off and the group will move on to repeat the performance elsewhere. Sometimes, the leader will stop at a likely spot and try to pish up a bird. Stand by quietly with binoculars at the ready and watch carefully for movement. Avoid pointing if you spot a bird — this tends to make it flush.

Field trips to wetlands areas with dike roads often take the form of caravans. Participants meet in the parking lot and form a line of cars that proceeds around the road, stopping at the turnouts. At each turnout, everyone piles out of the cars, sets up their spotting scopes, and begins scanning. Because these areas are flat, open, and tend to have monotonously similar vegetation (mostly phragmites), directions to a bird of interest can be even harder to follow, especially when they are expressed as "It's just to the right of the dowitcher." Fortunately, the leader will focus a spotting scope on the interesting birds and make sure everyone gets a good look.

An average field trip to a local birding area — one sponsored by your local bird club, for instance — gets underway between seven and eight o'clock in the morning. At the normal leisurely pace, the trip is over within two hours and covers no more than two miles of fairly easy walking. Field trips to see shorebirds tend to last longer because the birds are visible and active longer. Special excursions to hot spots can be all-day or even overnight trips because of the travel time involved.

As a trip participant, you should observe proper birding etiquette. Arrive on time for the start of the trip (although the trip is unlikely to start exactly on time). Leave dogs and young children home. Avoid doing anything that will frighten away or harm the birds — don't approach too closely, point, move abruptly, or speak loudly. If you see a bird, even if you can't identify it, alert the group, giving the most precise directions you can. Be careful not to step into anyone's line of vision, particularly if photography is going on. Stay with the group; don't get ahead of the leader. In a caravan, offer a ride to anyone who needs it and drive carefully. Share your spotting scope, your snacks, your tissues, and anything else. Be sure to thank the group leader at the end.

## DRESSING FOR THE FIELD

Your birding field trip starts when you get dressed at home. What you wear can make all the difference to your trip's success. Dress properly and you will have an enjoyable and productive excursion; dress improperly and you will be miserable.

### Footwear

Comfortable, broken-in footwear appropriate to the weather and terrain is essential to any birding trip. Birders do a lot of walking. You will very quickly regret wearing inappropriate, new, or ill-fitting shoes of any kind as your blisters rise and your spirits sink. For general birdwatching on ordinary trails, a comfortable pair of light hiking boots or walking shoes is usually sufficient. For more rugged terrain, heavier, ankle-high hiking boots may be in order.

Cold feet will quickly make you feel cold all over; cold, wet feet will have this effect even more quickly. In cold weather, wear warm socks, preferably made of wool or a wool blend. Wool has the significant advantage of retaining heat even when wet. A polypropylene liner sock is also a good idea. Insulated boots and shoes containing Thinsulate or the equivalent are lightweight, comfortable, and really do keep your feet warm.

Waterproof footwear is particularly desirable in the spring, when the trails are most likely to be wet and muddy. Leather footwear can be successfully treated with waterproofing substances. Muddy trails and trails covered with wet, fallen leaves can be treacherously slick. Good traction from the soles of your footwear is as important as water resistance.

Most good hiking boots are water-resistant at least to some degree, but solid rubber is the only material that really keeps the water out. Boots with rubber lowers and leather or synthetic uppers are effective. Another good choice is rubber Wellington boots worn with warm socks instead of — not over — shoes. A great advantage of Wellies is that they can be simply hosed off to get them clean.

## Hats

It's a good idea to wear a hat while birding. In cold weather, a hat greatly reduces heat loss from your head and helps keep you warmer longer. Be sure the hat covers your ears — frostbitten ears are no fun. In hot weather, a hat shades your head and helps keep you cool. In all weather, a hat keeps your head dry.

Select a hat that is comfortable, appropriate to the weather, snugly fitting, and with a brim to shade your eyes and keep precipitation off your face (particularly important if you wear eyeglasses). Wear a baseball-style cap with a long brim for extra shading in very bright situations — beaches, for example. The long bill can also be useful for steadying your binoculars if you want to gaze at something for an extended period. To do this, hold your binoculars to your eyes as usual, grasp the bill with your fingers, and hold it against the top of the binocs. This maneuver reduces arm fatigue and shaking.

## Clothing

Sturdy, comfortable clothing appropriate to the weather and the terrain is essential for a field trip. Birding is hard on your clothes, especially trousers and outerwear. You will often get wet, muddy, or worse. Select clothing that can survive rough treatment.

Dress for the weather. This does not mean the weather where you are when you get dressed—it means the weather where you will be when you are birding. An overcast but mild spring day with a refreshing breeze in the city is likely to be light rain, chilly temperatures, and a biting wind at the coastal refuge you are visiting. Always dress in easily removed layers. It is far, far better to arrive at your destination and take off your sweater than it is to get there and be cold with no recourse.

Novice birders are often shockingly unprepared for cold weather. Invest in good thermal underwear, heavy socks, wool trousers or lined blue jeans, thick sweaters, and a good hooded parka (preferably down-filled). In moderately cold weather, you can get away with thin gloves that let you focus your binoculars while wearing them. It is almost impossible to focus your binocs wearing thick, clumsy ski-type gloves. In really cold weather, try wearing thin silk gloves underneath down-filled mittens. Slip your hand out of the mitten to focus.

As you bundle up for cold weather, be sure you can move your arms freely. A parka that binds every time you lift your binoculars becomes very annoying very quickly.

In hot weather, wear loose, lightweight clothing, preferably made of cotton. Avoid shorts and sandals.

In all weather, carry a lightweight wind/rain shell. These fold up into small packages that fit easily into a pocket or pack. A tip for birders with long hair: Bring a hair clip. Wind-whipped hair in the eyes will seriously diminish your birding pleasure.

To reduce the chances of spooking the birds, avoid brightly colored clothing, anything adorned with reflective material (sequins, metal studs, etc.), and anything that clanks (jewelry, metal canteens, etc.). Go with muted, dark colors, earth tones, or even camouflage gear.

### Birding Vests

Birders like comfortable, efficient clothing with lots of big, easily accessible pockets. Several manufacturers make lightweight, sturdy birding vests that have pockets specifically designed to hold field guides, notebooks, checklists, pencils, film cans, camera lenses, handkerchiefs, sandwiches, snacks, hats, canteens, bird callers, and all the other essential paraphernalia of birding. Check nature stores and the ads in birding magazines for prices and availability.

Birding vests can be warm on hot days, and they don't fit very well over parkas. They can also make you look a little dorky or cause you to be mistaken for a fly fisherman — but you're a birder and don't care what people think. An adjunct or alternative to a birding vest is a hip pack. The larger sizes can easily accommodate a field guide and lunch with room to spare. You can use the pack's tie-down straps to carry a sweater or jacket.

### Sunglasses

Glare from the sun is a big problem for birders, since it reduces your perception of color and leads to eye fatigue and nasty headaches. High-quality polarized sunglasses are the obvious solution. If you wear prescription eyeglasses, get prescription sunglasses — snap-on sunglasses that cover your regular glasses can create annoying light reflections when you are using optics. They also add another layer of glass for the light to go through before it reaches your retina, leading to loss of brightness and accurate color perception.

A strap to hold your sunglasses or eyeglasses around your neck when you are not wearing them helps keep them from getting lost, although it may get entangled with your binoculars. The slight risk of strangulation is preferable to losing an expensive pair of glasses. If you wear prescription eyeglasses all the time, consider using a retaining strap to hold them in place while you are on a birding excursion. Nothing will stop you from seeing birds faster than a lost or broken pair of eyeglasses.

Glare from water or snow and ice is as hard on your eyes as glare from a sandy beach on a summer afternoon. Bring your sunglasses along throughout the year.

## Other items

With experience, you will develop your own assortment of useful odds and ends. You will, of course, be carrying a notebook, writing implement, and field guide. Plastic bags are handy for carrying botanical specimens and dead birds. They are also useful for protecting optics and other gear from water and dirt. Bring several. A large scrap of soft cloth or old towel is good for wiping off water and dirt from you and your equipment. A pocket knife is always a good tool to have. Always bring plenty of tissues — it may be long way to the nearest restroom.

## Food and drink

Birding makes people hungry and thirsty. If you're planning an all-day trip, bring a hearty lunch and plenty of snacks such as fruit (fresh and dried), cookies, and pretzels. You may find yourself eating a frozen sandwich in the winter. Try carrying it in an insulated container or bring something warm (stew or chili, for example) in a thermos instead. Don't forget a fork. In the summer, pack your food in an insulated container with frozen blue ice packs to keep it cool and unspoiled. Even on a short trip, bring along some snacks.

Always bring something to drink. Plain tap water in a thermos or canteen is the simplest and cheapest approach. Fruit juice or iced tea are also good. Avoid carbonated and alcoholic beverages — they will not quench your thirst. In cold weather, a thermos of hot tea or coffee is essential. Drink plenty of fluids in both very hot *and* very cold weather.

## HAZARDS TO BIRDERS

Birding is basically a safe activity with little likelihood of injury beyond the occasional blister or mosquito bite. The few minor hazards can be dealt with easily.

## Insects

If you are bothered by insects and other creepy-crawlies — if an ant in the pantry sends you into a cleaning frenzy, if you panic at the sight of a spider, if you can't bear to pick up an earthworm — you will have a problem becoming a proficient birder. Birds like to go where the bugs are, and birders like to go where the birds are. Try to take a philosophical attitude toward bugs — think of them as bird food. And remember, there are thirty million insect species. You're outnumbered by billions to one.

Biting insects such as mosquitoes, gnats, chiggers, fire ants, black flies, greenhead flies, and ticks may be bird food, but they are also pests of the first order. At a minimum, anoint yourself and your clothing — particularly your socks and trouser legs — with plenty of insect repellent containing DEET before the start of your field trip. Learn to recognize and avoid fire ant mounds, wasp nests, and similar obvious dangers.

If you are so dedicated to birding as to venture onto a salt marsh in midsummer, no amount of insect repellent and protective clothing will keep you from being bitten by greenhead flies, mosquitoes, and other noxious insects. Even if you are less foolhardy, as a birder you must simply learn to live with a certain number of itchy bug bites.

Ticks, however, are another story. Birders are at serious risk from such nasty tick-borne illnesses as Lyme disease and Rocky Mountain spotted fever. Ticks are brown, eight-legged, wingless arthropods that feed on blood — human, mammal, and avian. Ticks climb into low, brushy vegetation in mixed grassland areas and wait for a potential host to brush by them. (Ticks do not jump onto hosts; they do not drop out of trees and bushes.) The tick then bites into the host to get a blood meal. After it has fed, the tick drops off. Generally, you won't feel a tick bite until after the tick is gone. At that point, the site may become red and itchy; then again, it may not.

Two serious diseases are carried by ticks. Rocky Mountain spotted fever (which, despite its name, is not confined to the Rockies) is carried by the familiar dog tick (*Dermacentor variabilis*). Lyme disease is carried by the tiny deer tick (*Ixodes dammini*).

If you become ill after visiting a natural area, be sure to tell your doctor that you have been exposed to ticks. Ask to have your blood tested for possible tick-borne diseases. With prompt antibiotic therapy, quick recovery is likely.

Although most tick bites are absolutely harmless, a bout with Lyme disease or Rocky Mountain spotted fever will seriously cut into your birdwatching. Take no chances. Especially in the late spring and early summer when ticks are most common, wear ankle-high footgear, long sleeves, long trousers, and a hat. Tuck your trouser ends into your socks, tuck your shirt into your trousers, and button your cuffs. Select light-colored clothing so ticks can be easily spotted. Stay on and to the center of trails and avoid brushing against vegetation at the edges. Don't go into brushy or grassy areas without trails. Use plenty of insect repellent, particularly around the ankles.

If you have been in an area where ticks are prevalent, check your body and clothing carefully afterward. Hairy areas of the body, especially the head, are very attractive to ticks. Ticks found crawling on the skin or clothing should simply be removed before they can attach themselves. There is no risk here — the tick must embed itself before it can transmit the disease. If a tick does attach itself, remove it promptly. Use a pair of tweezers to grasp the tick on either side of the head, as close to the skin as possible. Pull gently but steadily to remove the tick. Apply antiseptic to the bite site and wash your hands thoroughly. You can ask your doctor to send the tick for testing to see if it is infected, but this is expensive and not completely reliable. Chances are that you'll be fine.

### Sunburn

You can get a sunburn while birding even on a cool day in early spring or late autumn. Use sunscreen of the appropriate sun-protection factor (SPF) for your skin. Apply your bug spray on top of the sunscreen. Be sure to put sunscreen on the back of your neck and hands. If you have a bald spot, cover it with a hat.

## Poison ivy and other noxious plants

It's almost impossible to avoid poison ivy, poison oak, and poison sumac if you're a birder. Poison ivy, in particular, is ubiquitous. Poison oak is a little less common, and poison sumac is generally found only in swampy areas in the eastern and southern United States. Only about half of all people who come into contact with these plants will develop an itchy, oozy rash — but you won't know which half you're in until it happens to you.

An old adage for avoiding poison ivy is "Leaves of three, let it be." Poison ivy plants can be vines or shrubs. They have green, lobe-shaped leaves arranged in clusters of three. In the autumn, you will see clusters of small, white berries under the leaves — an important food source for birds. Don't touch. All parts of poison ivy, poison oak, and poison sumac plants, even if dead, contain the oily resin that causes irritation. Poison oak plants are bushy, with leaves that grow in clusters of three. The leaves have indentations that make them resemble oak leaves. Poison sumac is a woody shrub or small tree. The leaflets grow in pairs along a stalk. Learn to recognize and avoid these plants.

## Hypothermia and frostbite

Birders, especially young children and older birders, are subject to hypothermia and frostbite because they may spend long periods of time outdoors in very cold weather — during a Christmas bird count, for example. Hypothermia is a dangerous and sometimes fatal condition caused by a drop in body temperature of more than 4°F (2°C). Prolonged exposure to cold and windy weather, especially if you are improperly dressed, is a good way to bring on hypothermia; so is getting wet, even if you are properly dressed.

Frostbite means that the skin and tissues beneath the skin have frozen. Your ears, hands, nose, and feet are most likely to become frostbitten.

Hypothermia and frostbite are serious medical conditions requiring prompt attention. The symptoms and treatment are described in any good first-aid manual.

### Heat exhaustion

If you spend a prolonged period outdoors in very hot weather and sweat heavily, heat exhaustion can occur. If untreated, heat exhaustion can lead to the much more serious—even life-threatening—condition known as heatstroke (sunstroke). Heatstroke requires emergency medical help. Study a first-aid manual to learn the symptoms and treatment for heat-related conditions.

### Lightning and severe weather

A sudden thunderstorm while you are visiting a beach, meadow, or other open area such as a golf course exposes you to the risk of a lightning strike. Head quickly for shelter if the sky begins to darken ominously, if you hear distant thunder, or if you see lightning. Do not shelter under a tree! Your car, however, is a safe spot if you can't get indoors. Lightning storms can be accompanied by dangerous hail. Take shelter. Heavy downpours can lead to flash floods and local flooding. Take common-sense precautions: Don't wade or drive into a stream or puddle if you can't see its bottom, and don't drive onto flooded bridges.

## Deer and the hunting season

Deer and birders tend to be active at the same times in the same places. This makes hitting a deer with your car a real possibility, especially at dawn or at dusk. If you see a deer on or near the road, stop if you can and wait for it to cross the road or go back into the woods. Where there is one deer, there are usually more. Wait at least a minute or two to see if any more come along.

Birders often feel antagonistic toward hunters, particularly waterfowl hunters. It's an understandable feeling, but one based on ignorance. Hunters have been and remain a major force behind the conservation movement. Hunting organizations have done a great deal to help preserve and restore wetlands — a good example is Ducks Unlimited's work with the Reifel bird sanctuary near Vancouver. In addition, licensing fees and duck stamp money are earmarked for conservation purposes. (Many birders also purchase duck stamps every year. These collectible items feature beautiful bird art.)

The real problem is that birders and hunters share the same territory — and that can be dangerous. During the hunting season, try to stick to places where hunting is forbidden. If you really must go into an area that may have hunters, don't wear your cammies. Adorn yourself with blaze orange, stick to the trails, and make noise. During the wild turkey season, never try to follow a turkey's call to its source. There's a good chance that what you are hearing is actually a hunter luring in a bird. You could be mistaken for a turkey, with tragic consequences.

## Personal security

As a group, birders are amazingly honest and generous. Whenever they find lost binoculars, cameras, field guides, even caps and canteens, they make a strenuous effort to get them back to their rightful owners. It is unlikely in the extreme that a birder would ever steal something from you. Birders, alas, are in the minority. Take some basic security precautions for yourself and your gear. Always lock your car and put the key in a secure pocket, preferably one with a buttoned flap, along with your wallet. Avoid leaving optics or their telltale cases in full view in the car. Put them in the trunk, under a seat, or toss a blanket over them.

# Further Adventures in Birding

$W$hen you become a birder, you become part of a well-organized network of like-minded individuals. Your opportunities to venture farther afield with your fellow birders are wide.

## BIRDING ORGANIZATIONS

Three organizations are particularly important to birdwatchers: the National Audubon Society, the American Birding Association (ABA), and the Cornell Laboratory of Ornithology. A number of states also have active, independent Audubon societies.

A conservation organization with more than 550,000 members, the National Audubon Society works toward the preservation and wise use of America's natural heritage. The society's roots go back to 1886, when George Bird Grinnell, editor of the magazine *Forest and Stream*, formed the first American bird association, the Audubon Society, to protest the wholesale slaughter of birds by market gunners for their meat and plumes. The organization he founded became the National Audubon Society in 1940.

The National Audubon Society today has more than 500 chapters and also staffs 10 regional offices and a public-policy office in Washington, D.C. (see Appendix B). Its national sanctuary system protects more than 250,000 acres, and hundreds of additional acres are protected by local chapters. The National Audubon

Society publishes the general nature magazine *Audubon* and the technical journal *American Birds* (see Appendix C).

A number of states have independent Audubon organizations not affiliated with the National Audubon Society. This confusing situation dates back to the start of the Audubon movement at the turn of the century, when numerous conservation organizations sprang up using the Audubon name. Many eventually coalesced into what is now the National Audubon Society, but some remained unaffiliated as state societies with their own local chapters, magazines, sanctuaries, and activities. To complicate matters further, the National Audubon Society has chapters in every state, including those with independent Audubons. Fortunately, peaceful coexistence and frequent cooperation seem to be the rule. Independent Audubons publish magazines and newsletters, sponsor field trips, lectures, birdathons, birding trips, and other activities. If you live in a state with an independent Audubon, join it.

The American Birding Association is a birding-only organization founded in 1982; it now has over 10,000 members, mostly in the United States and Canada. Many, but by no means all, ABA members are dedicated birders with a serious interest in listing and traveling to see birds. The ABA is the semiofficial arbiter of birding records, tracking and publishing listing records, and assessing rare-bird reports. The association publishes *Birding*, a bimonthly magazine with articles on bird-finding, identification, and equipment. It also publishes the lively monthly newsletter *Winging It*, which includes notes on rare birds, detailed bird-finding information, and tour information. The ABA sponsors an annual conference and numerous birding trips throughout the year. A major advantage of joining the ABA is member discounts on the very wide selection of high-quality optics and birding books, including finding guides for virtually everywhere, that are carried in the sales catalog.

The Cornell Laboratory of Ornithology in Ithaca, New York, was founded in 1955. The lab conducts a number of cooperative research projects such as the Nest Record Program. Participants find bird nests in the field and record information about them on data cards. The information is compiled and analyzed at the laboratory to provide a comprehensive picture of the distribution, nesting habits, and population trends of many species. The lab analyzes data from the Christmas Bird Counts, breeding bird censuses, and winter bird-population studies sponsored by the National Audubon Society. The lab also sponsors Project FeederWatch for backyard birders. Membership in the lab brings you discounts on the broad selection of books, recordings, and other bird-related materials and gifts from the Crow's Nest Birding Shop, along with a subscription to the quarterly magazine *The Living Bird*.

## BIRDERS WITH DISABILITIES

A physical disability is no handicap to birdwatching. Today, most public nature areas — parks, campgrounds, and wildlife sanctuaries — are fully accessible to wheelchairs, with ramps, wider doors, restroom facilities, paved nature walks and viewing areas, and other facilities. Many parks now have water access and even wheelchair fishing areas — excellent places for seeing shore and water birds.

At many of the best birdwatching sites, a mobility handicap is hardly a problem at all. For instance, the best way to bird many wetlands sanctuaries is to drive along the dike road. You can easily see numerous birds without ever getting out of the car, especially if you use a window-mounted spotting scope. The hawk-watching site at Cape May Point is right next to a large, flat, paved parking lot, making it easily accessible.

Birdwatching is as much listening as watching. Because of this, many visually handicapped people enjoy birds. An excellent booklet called *Birding: An Introduction to Ornithological Delights for Blind and Physically Handicapped Individuals* is available from the Library of Congress. The booklet contains a list of the many recordings of books about birds available through the library at no charge, as well as other information. For a free copy, call (202) 287-5100.

## ADDITIONAL READING

Your field guide is just the first of many birding books you will soon begin to accumulate.

Two useful books for young birders are the classic *How to Know the Birds*, by Roger Tory Peterson, and *Familiar Birds of North America*, a volume in the Audubon Society Pocket Guides series.

For more detail about birds in general, invest in some of the standard reference works. A good general book for beginners is *Reader's Digest Book of North American Birds*. A detailed, worldwide general reference such as *The Cambridge Encyclopedia of Ornithology* is a must. If you can afford it, subscribe to the outstanding new-species profile, *The Birds of North America*, now being issued serially by the American Ornithologists' Union. The magisterial works of Alexander Skutch, one of the finest bird observers ever (and certainly the most long-lived), should be read by every birder.

Somewhat old-fashioned in style and appearance, but still very valuable today, are Arthur Cleveland Bent's twenty *Life History* volumes. In the 1920s, Bent compiled species accounts of all North American birds from hundreds of observers, combined them with comments gleaned from the works of the great American ornithologists, and wove everything together with his own excellent observations and commentary. These books are now available in in-expensive paperback editions.

For practical birdwatching, a must-have book is *The Birder's Handbook*, by Paul Ehrlich, David Dobkin, and Darryl Wheye. This book bills itself very accurately as "the essential companion to your identification guide." The three-volume *Audubon Society Master Guide to Birding* set is also essential, particularly for its detailed discussion and illustration of field marks.

In a category by itself is Christopher Leahy's witty and informative book, *The Birdwatcher's Companion*. This volume contains, in encyclopedia form, entries on virtually every aspect of birds and birdwatching in North America. An enjoyable and instructive book full of useful tips is *The Complete Birder*, by Jack Connor. *A World of Watchers*, by Joseph Kastner, puts birding into historical perspective.

When you think you're ready to take on the challenges of gull identification and other complicated issues, *Advanced Birding* by Kenn Kaufman will be your bible. If hawkwatching appeals to you, read *Hawks in Flight*, by Pete Dunne, David Sibley, and Clay Sutton. For shorebirds, an outstanding reference is *Shorebirds: An Identification Guide to the Waders of the World*, by Peter Hayman, John Marchant, and Tony Prater. Excellent studies of other individual bird families such as ducks and owls have been published; they are far too numerous to list here. To identify nests and eggs, see *Birds' Nests* (eastern and western editions), by Hal Harrison.

The fascinating stories behind bird names are given in *Dictionary of American Bird Names*, by Ernest Choate and *A Dictionary of Scientific Bird Names*, by James Jobling.

If you are interested in feeding and attracting birds, read *The Birdfeeder's Handbook*, by Sheila Buff and *The Audubon Society Guide to Attracting Birds*, by Stephen W. Kress. To understand the behavior of your backyard birds, see the guides to bird behavior by Donald and Lillian Stokes.

Every year, numerous books about the joys of birds and birdwatching are published. When you can't go birding yourself, the next best thing is reading about it. The classic works of naturalists such as Aldo Leopold and Niko Tinbergen are still enjoyable and valuable today. The birding adventures of contemporary writers such as the inimitable Pete Dunne, Janet Lembke, Jonathan Maslow, and many others make excellent reading, especially on long winter evenings.

Birders inevitably accumulate assorted field guides on other aspects of natural history — rocks, wildflowers, trees, fungi, butterflies and moths, and bugs of every description. An excellent, well-illustrated introduction to practical techniques in natural history is *The Amateur Naturalist*, by Gerald Durrell. If you've always wanted to know the best way to dissect an earthworm, this is the book for you.

## Magazines and journals

The articles in birding and natural history magazines are an excellent way to learn more about birds. Magazines such as *BirdWatcher's Digest*, *Birder's World*, and *Wild Bird* carry interesting, entertaining, illustrated articles that are full of solid information without being too technical. *Birder's World*, in particular, features outstanding color photography. *Birding*, *American Birds*, and *The Living Bird* are more technical but still very accessible.

The ornithological journals such as *The Auk*, *Condor*, and *Wilson Bulletin* are much more serious. Don't be intimidated. You may not understand every nuance of the statistical data in an article, but you can certainly grasp the main points.

Local, state, provincial, and regional birding clubs and organizations all publish newsletters and magazines. A subscription is usually part of the membership fee. You too can experience the joys of authorship by writing an article for your bird club's newsletter.

For more information about birding magazines, see Appendix C.

## Finding bird books

The same instinct that drives birders to add species to their life lists also seems to make them lust after birding books. Any good bookstore will have a reasonable selection of field guides and some basic reference books, along with a few recently published general birding and natural history books. Many birding books, however, are too specialized to be carried by any but the largest general bookstores. Your local bookstore may be able to special-order these titles for you, or you may be able to get them through interlibrary loans or from the library of your local bird club. You can also check the sales catalogs put out by the ABA and the Crow's Nest Birding Shop. Booksellers who specialize in bird books—new, used, and rare—often advertise in birding magazines.

Subscriptions to the popular birding magazines are relatively inexpensive. You get subscriptions to *Birding* and *Winging It* by joining the ABA. You can get the other magazines by dropping heavy hints about gift subscriptions around your birthday and Christmas. Many local libraries get some natural history and birding magazines. Research libraries generally get all the technical journals. As with books, you can usually arrange to see these through interlibrary loans.

## BIRD PHOTOGRAPHY

Many birders are also serious photographers. They take pictures for a broad spectrum of reasons, but for many, the primary purpose is to capture the beauty of the birds. This is a very old impulse in humans — depictions of recognizable bird species have been found in paleolithic cave paintings that are nearly 20,000 years old.

For beginners, photographs taken in the field can be a helpful tool for identification and documentation, as well as being an introduction to an absorbing aspect of birdwatching. To take even a minimally acceptable picture of a bird, you will need a good 35mm single-lens reflex camera, a telephoto lens (at least 120 mm), and a lot of film (preferably color slide film); a tripod is strongly recommended. You may also want to invest in a camera adapter for your spotting scope.

If you are photographing the bird simply to have a record of it, or if you are documenting a rarity, do your best to take a good picture without worrying too much about artistic merit. Try to make the photo sharply focused, well lit, and properly exposed but, if that's not possible, just do the best you can. Even a poor photo is better than no picture at all, particularly when it comes to documenting rarities. If the bird cooperates, try to get as many shots as possible, concentrating on the field marks. If you can, try to get a shot that shows the bird near something that provides a natural scale for size comparison.

You will often encounter bird photographers at birding sites and on field trips. Be courteous. Don't stand or set up your scope in front of the camera. Stay away from a blind if you know it is occupied by a photographer. Above all, don't do anything that will flush the bird.

Serious bird photography as an art and science is far too complex for the scope of this volume. An excellent book on the subject is *The Nature Photographer's Complete Guide to Professional Field Techniques*, by John Shaw.

Birders often purchase study (duplicate) slides of birds for their own use or to put together slide talks for delivery at the bird club's weekly meeting. There are two good, inexpensive sources for study slides: the Visual Services department at the Cornell Laboratory of Ornithology (see above) and Visual Resources for Ornithology (VIREO — see Appendix B). Slides from these organizations are for your own noncommercial use only; they may not be reproduced. Write for catalogs.

## RECORDING BIRD SOUNDS

Recent advances in recording equipment have made it easier for birders to make their own recordings of bird sounds. The gear has become lighter and easier to use. It has also become less expensive, but it is not by any means cheap. At a minimum, recording requires a parabolic or shotgun microphone, headphones, and a portable, battery-powered, high-quality tape recorder. This minimal package could easily cost you a thousand dollars. A fairly high level of expertise is needed to use the equipment effectively. This intriguing area is so new to the amateur birder that there isn't much information available. An informative article on the topic by D.C. Wickstrom appeared in *Birding*, the journal of the ABA, in 1988. Another source of information is the ever-helpful staff of the Library of Natural Sounds at the Cornell Laboratory of Ornithology. The library houses the world's largest collection of bird sounds, contributed by amateurs and professionals from all around the world.

## HURT BIRDS

As you watch birds, you may encounter birds that are sick or injured. You may also encounter damaged nests and "abandoned" chicks. What should you do?

In the case of sick and injured birds, the answer almost always is to leave the bird alone and let nature take its course. Don't allow human notions of compassion to interfere with the great web of life —and death. As discussed elsewhere, it is against federal law to keep any protected bird in captivity or to treat it unless you are a wildlife rehabilitator licensed by the federal government and state authorities.

One possible exception to the rule of noninterference is when a large bird such as a hawk or owl is injured—hit by a car, for example. These birds can sometimes be treated successfully and returned to the wild. Unfortunately, far more often they cannot be fully rehabilitated, and must either be humanely destroyed or kept in captivity.

A number of wildlife rehabilitation centers have been established in North America. To find one near you, contact your local animal protection organizations, or write to: International Wildlife Rehabilitation Council, Box 3007, Walnut Creek, CA 94598.

Sometimes a nest full of eggs or chicks will fall out of a tree, usually after a period of high winds. Should you find such a nest, simply place it back into the tree, tying it in place with string if necessary. If you don't know which tree it came from, just pick a good spot in any nearby tree; the parent birds will find the nest.

Sometimes you will find an unfledged chick that has fallen out of the nest. If you can find the nest, simply place the chick back into it; if not, place the chick on a low branch as close to where you found it as possible. Birds have virtually no sense of smell, and the idea that a bird will abandon its young if it smells humans on them has no basis in fact. It is inadvisable and probably unnecessary to take the chick in and raise it yourself. This is an extremely demanding task that is almost certain to end in heartbreak and failure. A certain amount of unsuccessful nesting is a sad but normal part of avian ecology. Ornithologists estimate that, on average, only one nest in ten is completely successful.

Every now and then you, or more likely your young child, will come across a baby bird that appears to be abandoned. This is almost certainly not the case. Many birds leave the nest before they are fully fledged; the parent birds continue to feed and care for them. In all probability, a parent of the "abandoned" bird is nearby, waiting for you to leave. If you move away a few yards and quietly wait, you will hear the parent calling to the chick and its answering peeps. Keep watching and you may be rewarded and relieved by seeing the parent feed the chick.

## CHRISTMAS BIRD COUNTS

The first Christmas Bird Count began on Christmas Day in 1900, when Frank Chapman, curator of birds at the American Museum of Natural History for fifty-four years, organized twenty-five groups in the Northeast as a protest against the traditional holiday slaughter in which teams competed to see who could shoot the most birds in one day. Today the National Audubon Society sponsors its annual Christmas Bird Count every year from December 17 to January 3. This event enlists the aid of over 45,000 birdwatchers in every state, every province of Canada, and several countries in South America, Central America and the Caribbean islands. Participants spend an entire day, regardless of weather, censusing the birds in their designated count circle. Every bird that can be identified is counted and later reported to Audubon. Every year, some 1,200 different species are identified, and well over 74 million individual birds are counted by over 1,500 groups.

The data provide critical information about the winter distribution of resident bird species and allow researchers to track changes in bird populations and ranges. The Christmas Bird Count is organized by *American Birds*, which devotes a book-sized issue every year to analyzing the results.

Each count area is a unique circle 15 miles in diameter, encompassing about 175 square miles. Groups try to cover as much territory within the circle as possible within the 24 hours of a single calendar day. Not surprisingly, some groups devote weeks to planning the logistics in order to claim the longest list of birds. The record is 326, noted in the Atlantic Canal Area of Panama in 1986. Some counters have been known to travel by dogsled to find their birds. Those who are less adventurous and live within the count circle can participate in a more leisurely fashion by being feeder watchers, recording the birds that visit their bird feeders during the course of the count day.

To participate in a Christmas Bird Count, contact your local bird club, a local Audubon Society chapter, or write to the Christmas Bird Count Editor at *American Birds*. Many counts are held on a Saturday or Sunday; a modest fee of a few dollars is collected to help defray expenses.

## BIRDATHONS AND BIG DAYS

Birdathons are competitive birding events generally held between April 1 and May 30, depending on the peak spring migration at the particular locales. Sponsors pledge money for each bird a birdwatching team spots during the chosen 24-hour period; participants also compete for awards and donated prizes. The proceeds are used to help finance local birding projects and sanctuaries. The annual World Series of Birding, sponsored by New Jersey Audubon every spring, is probably the best-known birdathon, garnering extensive media coverage. Needless to say, the logistics and execution of a 24-hour birding expedition by a five-person team are exhaustive and exhausting.

Big Days also occur during the peak spring migration period, with the date varying according to locale. Participants in a Big Day try to see as many species as possible in a 24-hour period, but they are free to travel as widely as they wish within the period (aircraft may be used). Big Days are often organized by a group of birding friends or by local bird clubs; they are more local and informal than birdathons. Serious birders report their totals to the American Birding Association. The Canadian record for a Big Day is 205 species, set in Manitoba in April 1987. The United States record is 231 species, set in California in April 1978.

Beginning birders are sometimes intimidated by organized counting events. After all, the people who do them see more birds in a day than many beginners have on their life lists. The publicity given to some counts tends to give a distorted picture of birding, putting the emphasis on quantity, not quality. If you can, participate in a count. You'll contribute to a worthy cause, add to scientific knowledge, expand your birding horizons, and generally have a ton of fun.

## BIRDING EDUCATION

Formal—but still fun—instruction in birdwatching and ornithology is available through summer and vacation birding programs sponsored by a variety of organizations, including the Cornell Laboratory of Ornithology. Check the pages of the birding magazines for announcements. The nonprofit Elderhostel organization offers excellent, reasonably priced, short courses for older adults. You might also want to take the home-study course offered by the Cornell lab.

## BANDING AND TAGGING

Bird banding data are a crucial source of information about bird longevity, migration, and migration routes. Bands returned from such faraway places as France, Nigeria, and South Africa, for example, helped demonstrate the remarkable migration pattern of the Arctic tern, proving that this bird makes an annual round-trip flight of 25,000 miles from its nesting grounds near the Arctic Circle to its wintering grounds in Antarctica.

Bird banding operations in the United States and Canada are coordinated by the Bird Banding Laboratory of the U.S. Fish and Wildlife Service; a special federal license and often state or provincial permits are needed to be an authorized bird bander. Volunteers are always welcome, but are not allowed to handle the birds.

To band a bird, it must first be trapped, usually in a fine net called a mist net. The birds are carefully removed, identified, weighed, and examined for age, sex, and physical condition. A light aluminum band of the appropriate size is attached to the bird's leg and the bird is released. Some 97 percent of all the birds banded are never found again, but the information provided by those that are recovered is invaluable. Very small birds are the least likely to be seen again, while up to 10 percent of banded gamebirds may be recovered.

If you find a dead banded bird (or if you find a band in a raptor pellet), remove it and straighten it out. A serial number and the words "ADVISE BIRD BAND WRITE WASHINGTON, D.C. USA" can be seen. Send the band and a description of the circumstances to: Bird Banding Laboratory, U.S. Fish and Wildlife Service, Laurel, MD 20708.

If you find a band on a living bird, *do not* attempt to remove it—you might injure the bird. Carefully note the number on the band and release the bird.

In addition to banding birds on the leg, researchers sometimes tag or color-mark birds in other ways. You may see Canada geese with conspicuous neck bands at a wildlife sanctuary, for example, or note a bird with colored wing tags or leg bands. If you see a tagged bird, note the color and position of the tags, any visible numbers or letters, and the general circumstances of the sighting. Report your findings to the site office or your local wildlife agency; someone there probably knows which research project the tags belong to and how to forward the information.

## VOLUNTEERING

Ornithology is one of the few sciences where the observations and assistance of amateurs are welcomed. Numerous bird studies, censuses, counts, and surveys are always being carried on throughout North America. The underfunded researchers in charge will often be glad to receive any help you can give. You don't have to know much about birds, but you do have to be enthusiastic and willing to learn. Check with your local bird club, the biology departments of nearby colleges, local, state, and provincial wildlife agencies, and regional natural history organizations to find projects near you.

# Appendices

· · · · · · · · · · · · · · · ·

**APPENDIX A:** *American Birding Association Code of Ethics*

I.  Birders must always act in ways that do not endanger the welfare of birds or other wildlife.

- Observe and photograph birds without knowingly disturbing them in any significant way.
- Avoid chasing or repeatedly flushing birds.
- Only sparingly use recordings and similar methods of attracting birds, and do not use these methods in heavily birded areas.
- Keep an appropriate distance from nests and nesting colonies so as not to disturb them or expose them to danger.
- Refrain from handling birds or eggs unless engaged in recognized research activities.

II. Birders must always act in ways that do not harm the natural environment.

- Stay on existing roads, trails, and pathways whenever possible to avoid trampling or otherwise disturbing fragile habitat.
- Leave all habitat as it was found.

III. Birders must always respect the rights of others.

- Observe all laws and the rules and regulations which govern public use of birding areas.
- Practice common courtesy in our contacts with others. For example, limit requests for information, and make them at reasonable hours of the day.
- Always behave in a manner that will enhance the image of the birding community in the eyes of the public.

IV. Birders in groups should assume special responsibilities.

As group members, we will

- Take special care to alleviate the problems and disturbances that are multiplied when more people are present.
- Act in consideration of the group's interest, as well as our own.
- Support, by our actions, the responsibility of the group leader(s) for the conduct of the group.

As group leaders, we will

- Assume responsibility for the conduct of the group.
- Learn and inform the group of any special rules, regulations, or conduct applicable to the area or habitat being visited.
- Limit groups to a size that does not threaten the environment or the peace and tranquility of others.
- Teach others birding ethics by our words and example.

Reprinted by permission of the American Birding Association

APPENDIX B: *Birding Organizations*

**National Audubon Society**
NATIONAL HEADQUARTERS
700 Broadway
New York, NY 10003
(212) 979-3000

WASHINGTON, DC OFFICE
666 Pennsylvania Avenue SE, Suite 200
Washington, DC 20003
(202) 547-9009

REGIONAL OFFICES
*Alaska and Hawaii:*
308 G Street, Suite 217
Anchorage, AK 99501
(907) 276-7034

*Great Lakes* (Illinois, Indiana, Kentucky,
   Michigan, Minnesota, Ohio,
   Wisconsin):
692 North High Street, Suite 208
Columbus, OH 43215
(614) 224-3303

*Mid-Atlantic* (Delaware, Washington, DC,
   Maryland, New Jersey, Pennsylvania,
   Virginia, West Virginia):
1104 Fernwood Avenue, Suite 300
Camp Hill, PA 17011
(717) 763-4985

*Northeast* (Connecticut, Maine, Massachusetts,
   New Hampshire, New York,

Rhode Island, Vermont):
1789 Western Avenue
Albany, NY 12203
(518) 869-9731

*Rocky Mountain* (Arizona, Colorado, Idaho,
   Montana, Utah, Wyoming):
4150 Darley, Suite 5
Boulder, CO 80303
(303) 499-0219

*Southeast* (Alabama, Florida, Kentucky, Georgia,
   Mississippi, North Carolina, Puerto
   Rico, South Carolina, Tennessee):
102 East Fourth Avenue
Tallahassee, FL 32303
(904) 222-2473

*Southwest* (Louisiana, New Mexico, Texas,
   Guatemala, Mexico, Panama):
2525 Wallingwood, Suite 1505
Austin, TX 78746
(512) 327-1943

*West Central* (Arkansas, Iowa, Kansas, Missouri,
   Nebraska, North Dakota, Oklahoma,
   South Dakota):
210 Southwind Place, Suite 205
Manhattan, KS 66502
(913) 537-4385

*Western* (California, Guam, Nevada, Oregon,
   Washington):
555 Audubon Place
Sacramento, CA 95825
(916) 481-5332

## Independent Audubon Societies

AUDUBON NATURALIST SOCIETY OF THE
CENTRAL ATLANTIC STATES
8940 Jones Mill Road
Chevy Chase, MD 20815
(301) 652-9188

CONNECTICUT AUDUBON SOCIETY
118 Oak Street
Hartford, CT 06106
(203) 527-8737

FLORIDA AUDUBON SOCIETY
460 Highway 436, Suite 200
Casselberry, FL 32707

HAWAII AUDUBON SOCIETY
212 Merchant Street, Suite 320
Honolulu, HI 96813
(808) 528-1432

ILLINOIS AUDUBON SOCIETY
Box 608
Wayne, IL 60184
(708) 584-6290

INDIANA AUDUBON SOCIETY
Mary Gray Bird Sanctuary
RR 6, Box 163
Connersville, IN 47331
(317) 827-0908

MAINE AUDUBON SOCIETY
Gilsland Farm
118 US Route 1
Falmouth, ME 04105
(207) 781-2330

MASSACHUSETTS AUDUBON SOCIETY
South Great Road
Lincoln, MA 01773
(617) 259-9500

MICHIGAN AUDUBON SOCIETY
6011 West St. Joseph, Suite 403
Lansing, MI 48908
(517) 886-9144

AUDUBON SOCIETY OF NEW HAMPSHIRE
3 Silk Farm Road
Box 528-B
Concord, NH 03302
(603) 224-9909

NEW JERSEY AUDUBON SOCIETY
790 Ewing Avenue
Franklin Lakes, NJ 07417
(201) 891-1211

AUDUBON SOCIETY OF RHODE ISLAND
12 Sanderson Road
Smithfield, RI 02917
(401) 231-6444

## Other Organizations

AMERICAN BIRDING ASSOCIATION
Box 6599
Colorado Springs, CO 80934
(800) 634-7736

CANADIAN NATURE FOUNDATION
453 Sussex Drive
Ottawa, Ontario K1N 6Z4
(613) 238-6154

CORNELL LABORATORY OF ORNITHOLOGY
159 Sapsucker Woods Road
Ithaca, NY 14850
(607) 254-2400

INTERNATIONAL COUNCIL FOR BIRD
PRESERVATION
32 Cambridge Road
Girton, Cambridge CB3 0PJ
England
(0223) 277318

VISUAL RESOURCES FOR ORNITHOLOGY
(VIREO)
Academy of Natural Science
19th and The Parkway
Philadelphia, PA 19103
(215) 299-1069

APPENDIX C: *Periodicals for Birders*

*American Birds*
National Audubon Society
700 Third Avenue
New York, NY 10003
(212) 979-3000

*The Auk*
American Ornithologists' Union
c/o Division of Birds
National Museum of Natural History
Washington, DC 20560

*Birder's World*
720 East 8 Street
Holland, MI 49423
(616) 396-5618

*Birding*
American Birding Association
Box 6599
Colorado Springs, CO 80934
(800) 634-7736

*BirdWatcher's Digest*
Box 110
Marietta, OH 45750
(800) 879-2473

*The Living Bird*
Laboratory of Ornithology
Cornell University
159 Sapsucker Woods Road
Ithaca, NY 14850

(607) 254-BIRD

*WildBird*
Three Burroughs
Irvine, CA 92718
(714) 855-8822

*Wilson Bulletin*
Wilson Ornithological Society
c/o Charles R. Blem
Department of Biology
Virginia Commonwealth University
Richmond, VA 23284
(804) 257-1562

APPENDIX D: *Birding Hotlines*

The first rare bird alert, the Voice of Audubon, was begun in 1954 by the Massachusetts Audubon Society. Today, many National Audubon Society local chapters, local independent Audubon societies, and other birding organizations have birding hotlines — recorded messages announcing general birding conditions in the region and details on where to find any rare and unusual birds that have been reported. The messages are changed at least once a week and often more frequently. The information is often quite detailed; have pen and paper handy to note directions and phone numbers. The expense to you is only the cost of the phone call.

The North American Rare Bird Alert (NARBA) is a fee-based service sponsored by the Houston Audubon Society. It provides information about sightings of unusual birds throughout North America, not just in a particular state or region. The number to hear the recorded message is given only to subscribers. Funds from NARBA subscriptions go to support an extensive system of refuges on the upper Texas coast. For more information, call 1-800-458-BIRD.

Some birders take hotlines very seriously and will drop everything at a moment's notice and travel hundreds if not thousands of miles to see (or not to see, as the case often is), a rare bird. As a beginning birder, you might think that you would never succumb to the chasing urge. All chasers were beginners once.

**Birding Hotlines**
United States
**Alabama**
Statewide: (205)987-2730
**Alaska**
Statewide: (907)248-2473
**Arizona**
Phoenix: (602)832-8745

Tucson: (602)798-1005
**Arkansas**
Statewide: (501)753-5853
**California**
Arcata: (707)826-7031
Los Angeles: (213)874-1318
Monterey: (408)375-9122
Morro Bay: (805)528-7182

Northern California: (510)528-0288
Orange County: (714)563-6516
Sacramento: (916)481-0118
San Bernadino: (909)793-5599
San Diego: (619)479-3400
Santa Barbara: (805)964-8240
Southwest Sierra/San Joaquin: (209) 782-1237
**Colorado**
Statewide: (303)279-3076
**Connecticut**
Statewide: (203)254-3665
**Delaware**
Statewide: (215)567-2473
**District of Columbia**
Districtwide: (301)652-1088
**Florida**
Statewide: (813)984-4444
Miami: (305)667-7337
Lower Keys: (305)294-3438
**Georgia**
Statewide: (404)509-0204
**Idaho**
Southeast: (208)236-3337
**Illinois**
Central: (217)785-1083
Chicago: (708)671-1522
**Indiana**
Statewide: (317)259-0911
**Iowa**
Statewide: (319)338-9881
Sioux City: (712)262-5958
**Kansas**
Statewide: (913)372-5499
Kansas City: (913)342-2473
**Kentucky**

Statewide: (502)894-9538
**Louisiana**
Baton Rouge: (504)293-2473
New Orleans: (504)246-2473
**Maine**
Statewide: (207)781-2332
**Maryland**
Statewide: (301)652-1088
**Massachusetts**
Boston: (617)259-8805
Western region: (413)253-2218
**Michigan**
Statewide: (616)471-4919
Detroit: (313)477-1360
Sault Ste. Marie: (705)256-2790
**Minnesota**
Statewide: (612)827-3161
Duluth: (218)525-5952
**Mississippi**
Coast: (601)467-9500
**Missouri**
Statewide: (314)445-9115
Kansas City: (913)342-2473
St. Louis: (314)935-8432
**Montana**
Statewide: (406)721-2935
**Nebraska**
Statewide: (402)292-5325
**Nevada**
Statewide: (702)649-1516
Northwestern region: (702)324-2473
**New Hampshire**
Statewide: (603)224-9900
**New Jersey**
Statewide: (908)766-2661
Cape May: (609)884-2626

**New Mexico**
Statewide: (505)662-2101
**New York**
Albany: (518)439-8080
Buffalo: (716)896-1271
Cayuga Lakes Basin: (607)277-5455
New York: (212)979-3070
Rochester: (716)461-9593
Syracuse: (315)682-7039
**North Carolina**
Statewide: (704)332-2473
**Ohio**
Blendon Woods Metro Park: (614) 895-6222
Cincinnati: (513)521-2847
Cleveland: (216)321-7245
Columbus: (614)221-9736
Northwest region: (419)875-6889
Southwest region: (513)277-6446
Youngstown: (216)742-6661
**Oklahoma**
Oklahoma City: (405)373-4531
**Oregon**
Statewide: (503)292-0661
Southern region: (503)826-7011
**Pennsylvania**
Allentown: (215)759-5754
Philadelphia: (215)567-2473
Western region: (717)963-0560
Wilkes-Barre: (717)825-2473
**Rhode Island**
Statewide: (401)231-5728
**South Carolina**
Statewide: (704)332-2473
**Tennessee**
Statewide: (615)356-7636

Chattanooga: (615)843-2822
**Texas**
Statewide: (713)992-2757
Austin: (210)483-0952
Lower Rio Grande Valley: (210)565-6773
North Central region: (817)261-6792
San Antonio: (210)733-8306
Sinton: (210)364-3634
**Utah**
Statewide: (801)538-4730
**Vermont**
Statewide: (802)457-2779
**Virginia**
Statewide: (804)929-1736 and (301) 652-1088
**Washington**
Statewide: (206)526-8266
**Wisconsin**
Statewide: (414)352-3857
Madison: (608)255-2476
**Wyoming**
(307)265-2473

Statewide:
Canada
**Alberta**
Calgary: (403)237-8821
**British Columbia**
Vancouver: (604)737-9910
Victoria: (604)592-3381
**New Brunswick**
Provincewide: (506)450-3825
**Nova Scotia**
Provincewide: (902)852-2428
**Ontario**
Provincewide: (519)586-3959

Hamilton: (416)648-9537
Long Point Bird Observatory: (519) 586-3959
Ottawa: (613)761-1967
Sault Ste. Marie: (705)256-2790
Toronto: (416)350-3000 ext. 2293
Windsor/Detroit: (313)477-1360
Windsor/Pt. Pelee: (519)252-2473
**Quebec**
Western region (in French): (819) 778-0737
**Saskatchewan**
Regina: (306)761-2094

# Index

·······